M D Lennox

Clayton

Missouri

An Urban Story

Mary Delach Leonard *—with—* Melinda Leonard

Contemporary photography
— by —
Mark Scott Abeln

REEDY PRESS

St. Louis, Missouri

Reedy Press
PO Box 5131
St. Louis, MO 63139, USA

Library of Congress Control Number:
2012943928

ISBN: 978-1-935806-33-2

Please visit our website at
www.reedypress.com.

Design by Jill Halpin

Printed in the United States of America
12 13 14 15 16   5 4 3 2 1

Contents

Foreword

Since its beginning as the seat of St. Louis County government, Clayton has experienced a long, steady, and prosperous growth. Over time, it has become a vibrant hub of business activity and a recognized civic leader in the St. Louis region.

Words frequently used to describe Clayton include inviting, exciting, progressive, stable, and suburban—with an urban flair. The community's business districts are home to corporate titans, professional service firms, award-winning restaurants, and charming retail shops. Clayton's outstanding residential neighborhoods, most within walking distance of boutiques and cafes, provide a range of lifestyle choices, from single-family homes and condominiums to rental apartments.

The city is known for stellar municipal services, consistently rated at the highest levels on citizen surveys, and the public School District of Clayton, which ranks as one of the best in the country. Clayton's pedestrian-friendly atmosphere, parks, and public art contribute to a highly desirable destination experience for residents, daily workers, and frequent visitors. The community offers an exceptional quality of life, made possible through the cooperative efforts of involved residents, a philanthropic business community, and a trusted city government.

I am proud to be part of this premier community and honored to help create its recent history as well as plan for its future.

Linda Goldstein
Mayor of Clayton
2007-2013

Foreword

A community that thrives for one hundred years warrants reflection. What are the qualities that account for its enduring success? One is a record of resilience, an ability to reinvent itself and adapt to changes in the environment. Clayton did just that in 1913, when community leaders saw the need to organize as a municipality. That decision was a game-changer.

Through the decades, other transformative actions occurred, such as supporting park spaces, protecting stately neighborhoods, and investing in schools. When the suburban lifestyle surged in the late 1940s, Clayton welcomed retail businesses to create a downtown district as an economic engine for the community.

Clayton leaders both respond to market forces and lead the charge in identifying new priorities. With Vision 2013, the mayor and Board of Aldermen articulated goals for sustainability, community growth, and regional leadership. Always committed to integrity and high standards, the elected officials work closely with a talented, capable, and dedicated citizenry.

Recently, residential and corporate citizens stepped up to a new level of participation as collaborative private partners with the city. Thanks to the efforts of the Clayton Century Foundation, we celebrate significant community enhancements this year and present this publication in honor of the city's one hundredth anniversary of incorporation.

The book traces our tracks from small rural town to corporate center. People who live in great old cities around the world know their city's stories. I hope you will embrace ours.

Judy R. Goodman
Ward 1 Alderwoman
2003-2012
Chair, Centennial Celebration

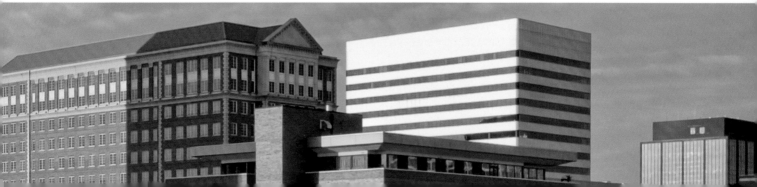

Acknowledgments

The authors acknowledge all who contributed their warm memories, invaluable expertise, and delightful memorabilia and photographs to this project, though we are humbly aware that this brief mention is in no way compensation for their generosity.

We begin by noting that this project was supported primarily by financial gifts from two prominent and historically significant members of the Clayton community: Washington University and the investment firm of Smith, Moore & Co.

We are grateful to members of the Clayton Century Foundation (CCF), for their financial support and guidance, and members of the Clayton History Society (CCF-History) who helped to launch the effort, in particular Ken Goldman and Steven Rosenblum, and those who contributed research material and read advance drafts of this manuscript: President Jim Sherby, Vice President Bob Paster, Secretary Rosemary Hardy, Treasurer John McCormick, Alderwoman Judy R. Goodman, Webmaster Cheryl Verde, Community Resource Coordinator Sarah Umlauf, Cindy Berger, Scot Boulton, Marie Casey, Jo Christner, Dan Human, Assistant Clayton Fire Chief Paul Mercurio, Liza Streett, and Rebecca Thorn.

Specifically, we note the tireless efforts of Scot Boulton, Judy R. Goodman, and Cheryl Verde, who led this book project, assisted by Sarah Umlauf and Parks and Recreation Director Patty DeForrest.

Our appreciation also is extended to the city's administration, which embraced Clayton's Centennial Celebration efforts and supported the development of this book project: Mayor Linda Goldstein, City Manager Craig S. Owens, City Clerk June Waters, and the Board of Aldermen: Judy R. Goodman, Andrea Maddox-Dallas, Michelle Harris, Cynthia Garnholz, Steven E. Lichtenfeld, and Mark Winings.

We are grateful to the following people who shared with us their personal perspectives on the city's growth after World War II: Clifford James, city manager from 1965 to 1976; Lee Evett, city manager from 1976 to 1991; and Douglas Geldbach, who worked for the city for thirty-four years, starting in 1959, directing the building and planning department through crucial development years.

The reference material used to write this book was collected from a variety of sources, most notably: the city of Clayton, which provided both historical and contemporary information; the archival collections of the Historic Hanley House and the Clayton Century Foundation–History and its website, www. claytonhistorysociety.org; the St. Louis County Library; the Missouri History Museum; and the National Register of Historic Places.

Our thanks to local historians, whose research provided valuable insight as we produced this work. In particular, we would like to thank St. Louis County Historian Esley Hamilton; James Sherby, the author of *From New Madrid to Claverach* (Virginia Publishing, 2009); Kathryn Bartlett Sinn, Washington University graduate, for her overview of Clayton architecture; Amanda Hassler and Jessica Laney, Leadership Clayton 2009; along with Christy L. Redmond, Casey Communications.

While we have noted sources throughout the narrative of the manuscript, this is a list of works most frequently referenced:

* Dickson Terry, *Clayton: a history* (St. Louis: Von Hoffman Press, 1976). Terry, a former *St. Louis Post-Dispatch* reporter, was commissioned by the city to produce a comprehensive history. Terry's 300-page narrative is a detailed chronicle that served as an insightful guide to this current work.

* Sarah J. Umlauf, *Westward Migration and Southern Alignment: The Joining of Two Virginians in St. Louis County*; a history of the Hanley family.

* William L. Thomas, *History of St. Louis County, Missouri* (St. Louis: S.J. Clarke Publishing Co., 1911).

* "Grandmother Lived in Clayton," *The Bulletin*, Missouri Historical Society, October 1952; a letter from Friederika Rauchenstein to great-grandson William C. Herbert, dated January 26, 1948.

* "Images of Our Community, Clayton," Wydown School, 1976; a collection of interviews of Clayton residents by the school's students.

* *The Clayton School District: A History of Excellence*; a booklet written by Friends of the Clayton School District, 2000.

* *The Story of Clayton; by the Boys and Girls in the Seventh and Eighth Grades of the Clayton Public Schools*; booklet produced in 1931.

* C. Kenneth Thies, "Clayton, Its Court House, Winner Take All." Mayor Thies delivered this speech at the annual meeting of the Clayton Chamber of Commerce, November 22, 1965.

* Earl W. Kersten Jr. and D. Reid Ross, "Clayton: A New Metropolitan Focus in the St. Louis Area," *Annals of the Association of American Geographers*, December 1968.

* Judy Kekich, "Clayton: The St. Louis County Seat Approaches Its Centennial," *Missouri Municipal Review*, September 2011.

* *The Clayton 1776 Fair: July 3 and 4, 1976, Shaw Park*; a booklet published by the Clayton Rotary Club.

* J. Thomas Scharf, *History of Saint Louis City and County from the Earliest Periods to the Present Day* (St. Louis: L.H. Everts, 1883).

* Robert A. Cohn, "The History and Growth of St. Louis County, Missouri"; a research document produced by St. Louis County in the mid-1960s.

* Calculations for determining the current value of historic dollar amounts were made by using the MeasuringWorth website, founded by Lawrence H. Officer and Samuel H. Williamson, economists at the University of Illinois at Chicago.

* We have cited the publication dates of news stories cited but would also like to thank the reporters of the day who were rarely given bylines for the reports we used from the *Watchman-Advocate*, *St. Louis Post-Dispatch*, *St. Louis Star-Times*, and *St. Louis Globe-Democrat*.

Aerial view of Clayton, 1955

Introduction

When Clayton was granted a city charter on April 7, 1913, the seat of St. Louis County finally began to figure out what kind of place it should be.

There were no fireworks. No parade or clanging of church bells to celebrate the birth of this new city that could look to its east and see urban development from St. Louis, Missouri, heading its way. By all accounts, it was business as usual on that Monday for Clayton residents who for thirty-five years had lived and worked in the little community that grew up around the St. Louis County Courthouse. As the local newspapers pointed out, the people of Clayton had shown little interest in making their community a real municipality until reports surfaced that neighboring University City might annex them.

"Until the citizens had the place incorporated a few days ago, Clayton was not even a village," the *St. Louis Post-Dispatch* wrote in a lengthy story on April 21, 1913. "It was just a place, a part of St. Louis County with no government save that of the county. The people liked that condition of things and had no desire to become a city until they got good and scared . . ."

Clayton finally had an identity—and a mayor and aldermen appointed by the St. Louis County Court as part of the incorporation process. They were all familiar faces—longtime residents who had been helping to run the place. When something needed fixing, the neighbors and business owners of Clayton pitched in to fix it. After a fire threatened the town, they banded together to start a volunteer fire department. When the population grew, it was time to build a one-room schoolhouse.

Clayton was born of the Great Divorce between St. Louis City and St. Louis County in 1876, and it took a while for the new county seat to make something of itself. A quarter of a century had already passed when the world came to nearby Forest Park to see the mind-boggling exhibits of the 1904 World's Fair, but the town wasn't ready to cash in on the hoopla. As Dickson Terry wrote in *Clayton: a history*, the citizens of Clayton had some big ideas early on regarding the fair, but little came of them. Progress in Clayton kept to a slower pace in those days.

Based on newspaper accounts of the incorporation process, it is safe to say that, when push came to shove, Clayton's citizens stood together. That same spirit would see the community through the changing—often trying—times ahead. In April 1913, the nation had a new president—Woodrow Wilson—and Missouri had a new governor—Elliot Woolfolk Major. There were rumblings of political discontent in Europe, but it would be four years before any of Clayton's young men would be sent "over there" to fight in World War I. In the decades that followed, the city would make slow but steady progress before taking a roller-coaster ride with the rest of America through the Great Depression, followed by a second world war. Only then would the city truly come into its own.

During research for this book, it was evident that Clayton residents have always shared a deep fondness for their "home place" and that they are willing to work together to get things done. In an interview for this project, Lee Evett, who served as city manager from 1976 to 1991, emphasized the spirit of cooperation he observed among the city's elected officials. "They didn't always agree with each other. Sometimes they violently disagreed with each other, but they all liked each other," Evett said. "So when the disagreement was over, they were back to liking each other. To be blunt, I've never seen it in another city. Often, people carry their professional prejudices into their personal lives. In Clayton, they had their professional prejudices, but they didn't let them interfere with getting the job done. That sense of solidarity continues to be a unique characteristic of Clayton's Board of Aldermen and is a fundamental element in maintaining the city's preeminence."

From the outset, we have considered this project to be a museum exhibit presented in book form: a timeline of memories, events, and facts, illustrated by pictures, old and new. Although Clayton's history dates to pioneer days, this book concentrates on the years after incorporation and on the community's history, rather than on the history of St. Louis County. But even so, a century is a long period to cover in a book of this length. Just as a museum exhibit is limited by space, we recognized that this book could not mention every place and event, or every business, civic, religious, or educational leader who contributed to the city's history. Still, we hope that these snippets and pictures provide at least a sense of how the people of Clayton first rose to the occasion one hundred years ago and have worked together ever since to advance their community.

It is always amusing to look backward from the present to imagine the old days. But it is even more fun to imagine the residents of early Clayton looking upon the present. Think of George Autenrieth gazing out the window of his hotel across from the county's first courthouse that was constructed in 1878; today, he would look upon a modern, multi-floored county government complex, surrounded by high-rises that tower over the one hundred acres of land that Ralph Clayton donated for a county seat.

He would see that Clayton has become quite a "place."

Mary Delach Leonard and Melinda Leonard

Clayton

Missouri

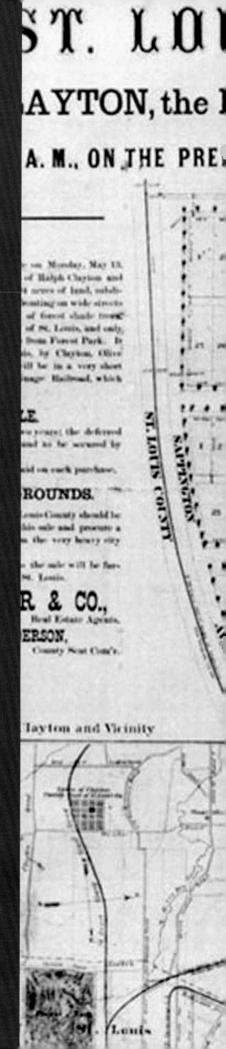

Chapter One

Rise and Shine:
In 1913, Clayton wakes up and becomes a city

In June 1913, Charles Fiedler, an old and respected resident of Clayton, "walked up and planked down a dollar" for a dog license, the first revenue collected by the brand new city. The occasion was so noteworthy that it was detailed on the front page of the *Watchman-Advocate*, the weekly newspaper that reported on the comings and goings in the small Missouri community of just under two thousand that served as the county seat of St. Louis County.

S COUNTY PROPERTY!

County Seat, Thursday, June 6th, 1878.

TITLE PERFECT.   Warranty Deeds given by the County.

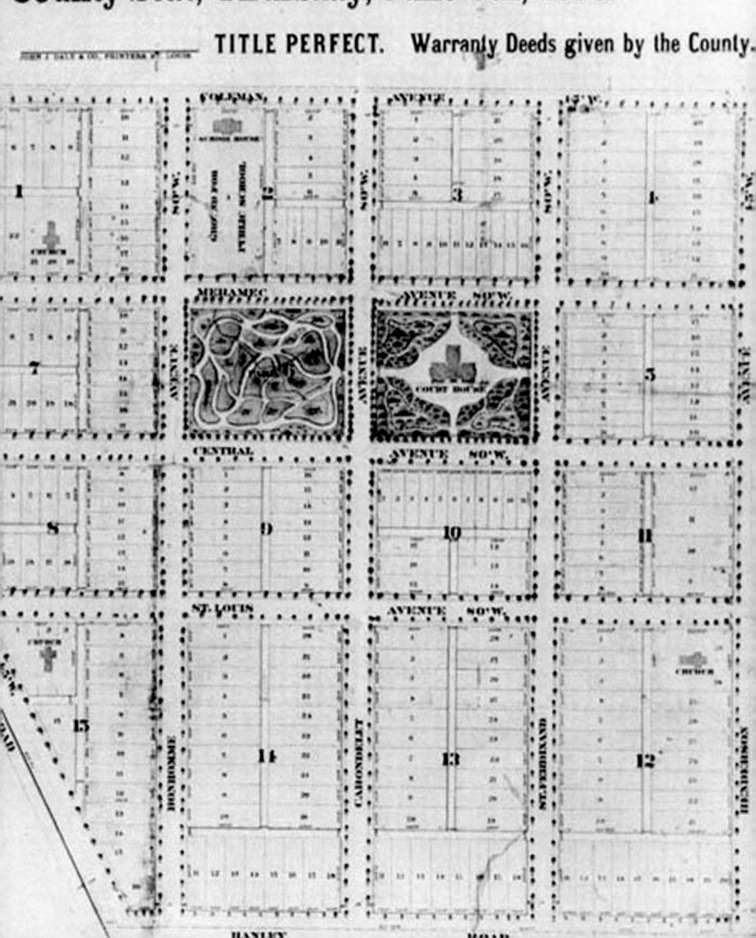

Saving "Salty's Bacon"

Why did the newly appointed city officials place a tax on dogs—one dollar on males and two dollars on females—as the city's first revenue source in 1913? According to the newspapers and the personal histories of Clayton's early citizens, the community had gone to the dogs.

Mrs. F. W. Rauchenstein, whose memoirs were published by the Missouri Historical Society in 1952, put it this way: "We seldom went out at night, except for some special occasion, because we had few sidewalks, and they were just planks, and no light at all. We carried a lantern with us so as not to fall, or bump into some person, or a horse or a dog. Horses, cows, and lots of dogs were allowed to run loose."

Townspeople had a soft spot for at least one stray, according to the *Watchman-Advocate*. On June 6, 1913, the newspaper related the tale of Salty, a "popular specimen of dogology" abandoned by a resident who left

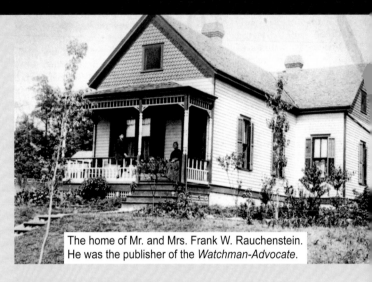

The home of Mr. and Mrs. Frank W. Rauchenstein. He was the publisher of the *Watchman-Advocate*.

Clayton to start a saloon business in a nearby town. According to the newspaper, Salty had narrowly "escaped a séance with the dog catcher" thanks to the intervention of the proprietor of the Clayton Pool Parlor who started a fund on the pooch's behalf. "It was not long until ten friends of the purp (cq) had contributed 10 cents each in raising the license fee," the newspaper reported, adding that the dog's tag was to be engraved with the names of all ten donors who saved "Salty's bacon."

The first ordinance in the city of Clayton authorized the taxation of dogs (203 Linden Avenue, circa. 1910).

"Clayton is no longer penniless," the *Watchman-Advocate* announced in its June 6, 1913, edition. "Not a dollar was deposited in the treasury from the time the town was incorporated the first week in April until after the ordinance authorizing the taxing of dogs went into effect on June 1." Other residents also stepped forward to pay the tax, and soon City Collector Henry Stecker amassed a "snug sum."

Although its city charter was brand new, the village of Clayton was nearly four decades old when Fiedler contributed that first tax dollar to the municipal treasury. The community traces its roots

Ralph Clayton

In 1877, Clayton donated one hundred acres of farmland to St. Louis County for a new county seat. Clayton, who was born in Virginia in 1788, was a prominent landowner in the county who for a time operated a tannery on his farm and served as a justice of the peace. The town, named for Clayton, was less than six years old when he died in 1883.

Martin Franklin Hanley

Hanley was born in Virginia in 1814 and migrated to St. Louis County in 1834, where he opened a blacksmith shop and sold farm implements. He and his wife, Cyrene Clemens Hanley, contributed four acres of farmland to the creation of the county seat. The acreage donated by Clayton and the Hanleys comprise what is now considered the downtown business district of Clayton. Hanley's two-story farmhouse, built in 1855, is owned by the city and preserved as a museum.

to 1876 and the contentious special election that approved the "divorce" of the county and the city of St. Louis. The town took its name from farmer Ralph Clayton, an early settler of the area who donated the bulk of the land for the new county seat. Clayton supplied one hundred acres; his neighbors Martin Franklin and Cyrene Hanley also contributed four acres.

In its early years, Clayton was a small settlement of homes and businesses surrounding the St. Louis County Courthouse square, as described by William L. Thomas in his 1911 *History of St. Louis County*. The community grew up around the grand two-story brick courthouse—with its impressive cupola and shaded lawn—constructed in 1878 at a cost of $38,000. Although Clayton grew slowly at first, Thomas noted that the town eventually evolved from a "dull and uninteresting place" into a "political mecca" and "attractive suburban town." While some

The original Clayton courthouse, 1907

The St. Louis County *Watchman-Advocate*, published every Friday, covered county government and news—big and small—of local interest. It was the official organ of the Republican Party.

Claytonians were drawn to the community by business opportunities, others lived there out of necessity because they represented constituencies from remote areas of the county—too long a commute in the horse and buggy days of the early twentieth century.

By Thomas's count, Clayton was home to a dozen or more distinguished attorneys, four physicians, and two dentists. Businesses included two barbershops, three newspapers, two financial institutions, a dry goods store, a saddlery, two hardware stores, three groceries, a bakery, three restaurants, two poolrooms, two saloons, and one hotel. The town also had its own post office and a volunteer fire department.

Under the heading "Wake up! It's Gettin' Up Time!" Thomas described a growing sentiment that the town should incorporate and collect taxes to fund improvements in public services: transportation, fire and police protection, sanitary conditions, and the building of more granitoid sidewalks. "Notwithstanding the patent fact that Clayton is cosmopolitan in size as well as in character of its residents and floating frequenters, there are citizens of the town who think that its magnitude demands a definite boundary."

By 1908, the *Watchman-Advocate* was also noting talk of incorporation and frequently reminding readers that the growing community was "the only county seat in Missouri without municipal government." On June 28, 1912, the newspaper reported a building boom totaling nearly $150,000. Among the projects: an addition to the courthouse, several residences, the laying of the cornerstone for a new St. Joseph's Catholic Church, a new Masonic Hall, and new buildings for the St.

Did you *Know?*

At the time of Clayton's incorporation, the St. Louis County Court was the governing body that managed county business. Despite its title, it was not a judicial body but served as a board of supervisors. The members of the court in 1913 were Presiding Judge John Wiethaupt and Associate Judges William Buermann and Albert A. Wilmas.

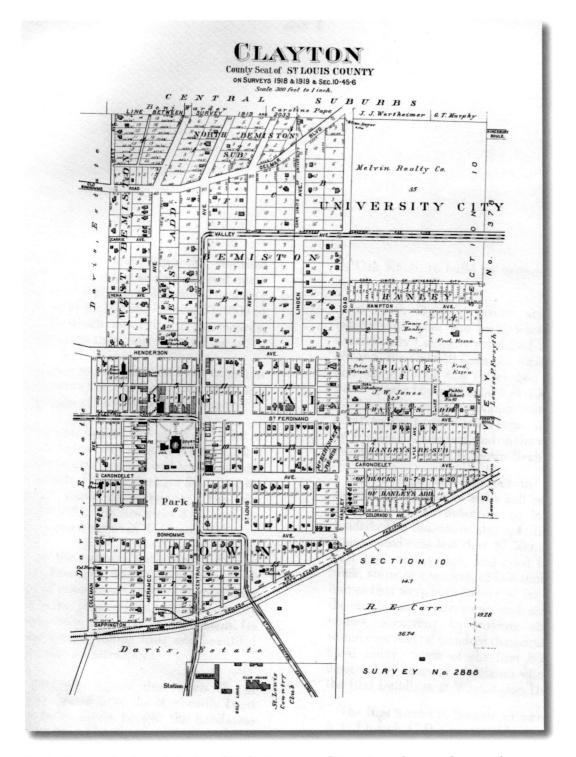

CLAYTON
County Seat of ST LOUIS COUNTY
ON SURVEYS 1918 & 1919 & SEC. 10-45-6
Scale 300 feet to 1 inch.

Louis County Bank and the Land Title Company. "There is no better place to observe general activity in building circles than right here in Clayton," the paper argued.

Not surprisingly, residents responded swiftly in December 1912 when reports surfaced that neighboring University City had plans to annex part of their community. They feared that University City could call a special election and vote to extend its limits, leaving Clayton residents with nothing to say in the matter. On December 18, 1912, approximately seventy-five Claytonians gathered at the county courthouse for an emergency meeting to discuss a plan of action.

CLAYTON MARRIAGE MART ENJOYS BOOM

The local newspapers often referred to Clayton as a "Gretna Green"—a reference to a Scottish city known for elopements—because the county seat was a popular wedding destination. On July 4, 1913, the *Watchman-Advocate* reported that nearly 1,500 couples got their marriage licenses at Clayton each year, making it the largest marriage market outside of the state's big cities. That June, 134 couples were married at the county courthouse, 22 more couples than the previous year. Said the newspaper:

Many of the couples licensed at Clayton seek romance and often come out from the city in taxicabs or carriages bedecked with white ribbons and drawn by white steeds. There has been enough rice spilled on the sidewalks and in the corridors of the Courthouse at Clayton to seed a full crop of this cereal in Imperial Japan. Enough old shoes to keep a regiment of soldiers shod for a year have been cast promiscuously about, and enough champagne has been toasted "to the bride" to float a battleship.

The *Watchman-Advocate* detailed the drama two days later in a one-column story on the front page. The story stated that interested residents had taken definite action and that Clayton "is to be incorporated. The mayor of Clayton will soon blossom forth in all his glory, invested with legal authority, and the municipal assembly of the county seat will wrestle with problems that naturally come with the founding of a new city of the fourth class—and all because University City has evil designs on the taxable wealth of Clayton." The paper noted that Clayton's citizens wanted no connection to E. G. Lewis, the controversial promoter and magazine publisher who founded University City and served as its first mayor. The *St. Louis Post-Dispatch* also reported on the meeting but noted, "Mayor E. G. Lewis of University City denied there is any intention of annexing a part of the county seat."

The incorporation committee moved quickly, with C. C. Crossman, president of the newly formed Clayton Welfare Association, serving as chairman. Other participants included attorney Julius R. Nolte and former associate county judge Fred L. Kerth, both of whom would later serve as mayors. Nolte told the

Watchman-Advocate that the committee planned to present the county court with an incorporation petition bearing the names of the majority of taxable inhabitants within the boundaries of the proposed municipality. The committee also mapped out the proposed new city.

Approximately three hundred residents turned out for a second public meeting on January 25, 1913. The *Watchman-Advocate* noted that the "earnestness" of the participants at the Saturday night meeting served as evidence that the town's incorporation would meet with general favor. Residents approved a plan to divide the proposed town into four wards and agreed to recommend to the county court a slate of city officers headed by William F. Broadhead, a prominent attorney who would serve as mayor.

The Clayton City Hall was designed by architects Maritz and Young and dedicated on July 2, 1931.

The petition to incorporate was filed with the county court the following Monday—January 27, 1913—by Fred J. Hollocher, cashier of the Trust Company of St. Louis County, who served as secretary at the mass meeting. An examination of the tax books found 315 personal taxpayers within the proposed boundaries, and the county assessor's office appointed two attachés to verify the signatures on the petition.

On April 7, 1913, the county court granted Clayton a charter. From start to finish, the town incorporated in just three months, prompting the *Post-Dispatch* to comment in a story published that day: "It all happened Monday in the St. Louis County Court, that potent body which isn't really a court at all, but a board of supervisors. The 'judges' granted the local Welfare Association's petition for incorporation, and named a Mayor and a complete set of officials for the new city, all just as easy and informal as a Clayton wedding."

A half-century later—in November 1965—C. Kenneth Thies, Clayton's mayor from 1946 to 1952, summed up the good fight in a speech to the Clayton Chamber of Commerce. Thies compared Clayton's birth to baseball executive Branch Rickey's description of baseball as a "game of inches." He cited instances in which Clayton's existence had also come down to "inches"—close calls that could have gone either way.

Thies noted the first crucial moment was the vote to separate St. Louis City and St. Louis County. The initial tally found that the measure failed in the special election held on August 22, 1876. After supporters alleged fraud, however, a recount was held. Four months later—on December 29—the St. Louis Court of Appeals announced that the city-county separation had been adopted by a majority of 1,253 votes. "By an astonishing recount, Clayton avoided becoming merely a west-end subdivision of St. Louis," Thies said.

The former mayor suggested that Clayton's second close call came during voting over the location of the new county seat. In addition to Ralph Clayton's donation of farmland, several cities in the county offered alternate proposals, including Florissant (in what was then St. Ferdinand Township) and Kirkwood. Clayton's proposal was approved by just eighty-seven votes, and Thies speculated that it was lawyers who nudged the vote in Clayton's favor. "Knowing lawyers as I do," Thies said, "I have the hunch that the lawyers banded together and concluded that if they were going to practice law in both the city of St. Louis and St. Louis County, it was only a half-day's ride, either horseback or by buckboard, from downtown St. Louis to Ralph Clayton's farm, whereas it was probably a full-day's ride by either horseback or buckboard up to Florissant or over to Kirkwood."

Thies also offered an intriguing account of Clayton's race to incorporation:

The year was 1913 and Clayton is a little cluster of houses around the Court House, wholly unincorporated as a town and Ed Lewis and his boys over in University City, who had incorporated University City with a great splash in 1906, decided that it would be to their interest to annex Clayton and make it a subdivision of University City. These gentlemen proceeded with their legal papers for annexation, but they made only a slight mistake. They let the word get out. On the morning, when at 9 a.m. they filed papers for annexation, they discovered to their dismay that five or six Claytonians had sat up most of the night preparing incorporation papers and that these papers had been filed just about an hour before the annexation papers had been filed and thereby preempted the matter legally.

The *Watchman-Advocate* and the *Post-Dispatch* chronicled every step leading to Clayton's incorporation; however, their accounts don't mention the dramatic

THEN and NOW

1913

Total population of Clayton: 1,948

Land area: About 110 acres

Source: City Collector Henry Stecker's census, taken on foot after incorporation; *Watchman-Advocate*, November 28, 1913.

2010

Total population of Clayton: 15,939

Land area: 2.5 square miles

Source: The 2010 U.S. Census

The in/out daytime population: Approximately 46,000 people commute daily to work and shop in Clayton, the seat of St. Louis County and a thriving hub of metropolitan St. Louis.

One of the saddest days in Clayton history was August 30, 1920, when Benjamin Corner, the city's third marshal, and Eugene Conrey, a St. Louis County deputy sheriff, were killed while making midnight rounds in Conrey's Model T Ford. The lawmen were shot while investigating a car stopped near the intersection of Jackson Avenue and Forsyth Boulevard. Willis Millard and George Parr were charged and convicted of murder. The *Watchman-Advocate* reported that the funerals for the slain officers were the largest ever held in St. Louis County. The newspaper also led a fund-raising effort to assist the families of the fallen officers.

Benjamin Corner

all-night vigil described by Thies. The *Watchman-Advocate* commended residents for keeping "their eyes open" to preserve their community, while the *Post-Dispatch* noted that the incorporation petition was signed by almost everyone in Clayton because if the town was to have a city government it wanted one of its own.

The first meeting of the city fathers was held on April 16, 1913, at Mayor Broadhead's law offices. Initial tasks included writing ordinances to appoint a city attorney, street commissioner, and city clerk—and identifying sources of tax revenue. "It will require some time before the municipal machinery is properly oiled and in good working order," the *Watchman-Advocate* noted, "but Clayton has a fine set of officers and they are beginning their labors with the view of improving all conditions, protecting and promoting at the same time the best interests of all the people."

CLAYTON BECOMES REAL CITY AND HAS ITS FIRST MAYOR

One of Clayton's first houses, at right, was built in 1880 for William F. Broadhead, who became Clayton's first mayor in 1913.

BY THE NUMBERS

Monthly pay for Clayton firefighters, 1917

$90 – Assistant Chief Adolf Hoffman, who was also the city's building inspector

$60 – Professional firemen (there were two)

$50 – Driver of the fire engine

$25 – Chief A. W. Schmid, who was also judge of the county probate court

$2 – Fire marshal, monthly

PROFILE
SAFEGUARDING THE CITY

An important sign that the new city of Clayton was making progress came in March 1917 when the Clayton Board of Aldermen established the Clayton Fire Department as a professional department. Until then, the firemen were all unpaid volunteers.

Until the city incorporated there was no tax revenue to fund municipal services, such as police and fire protection. The St. Louis County sheriff provided law and order, but residents were on their own for fire protection. That changed after a fire on March 20, 1897, threatened to destroy businesses on the town square. According to the *Watchman-Advocate*, neighbors pitched in to fight the early morning blaze at Schweighofer's Bakery on Meramec Avenue, carrying water from nearby cisterns in whatever containers they could find. Fearing the fire would spread, they emptied the buildings next door, hauling furniture and merchandise onto the courthouse lawn. George Autenrieth, one of the few townspeople who had a telephone, called the St. Louis Fire Department. It took forty-five minutes for the two fire engines to arrive from the city, but the fire was contained to the bakery.

Disaster was averted, but it was a wake-up call to the citizens of the county seat. A few weeks after the fire, Autenrieth held a meeting at his hotel to discuss buying a fire engine and recruiting volunteers. The town's new fire committee bought a Rex Double Cylinder and Chemical Engine and paid for it with subscription fees collected from residents.

The *Watchman-Advocate* reported that nearly forty men signed up for Clayton's new volunteer fire department. Their reward would be silver badges "pinned on

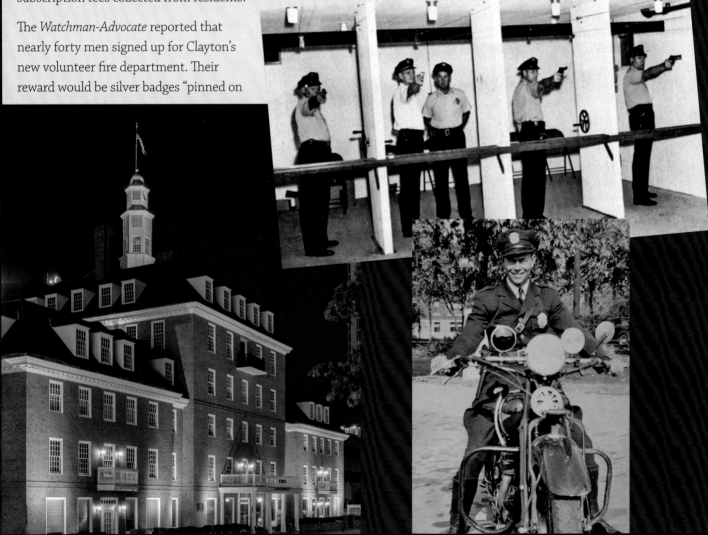

their manly bosoms." They had their work cut out for them. The new fire apparatus wasn't motorized, so when a fire broke out the firemen would commandeer a horse from a nearby stable to pull it, according to Dickson Terry's history of Clayton. Their efforts were also hampered by a limited supply of hose and fireplugs. Their ladder truck was a converted beer truck with one ladder. In 1915, residents approved a bond issue for $10,000 to buy a motorized Robinson pumper. But until 1924 when the city built a firehouse at 7755 Forsyth, the firemen made do in makeshift facilities, storing their equipment first at the courthouse and later at Arthur Kerth's garage at 31 North Meramec, the first filling station in town.

Today, the Clayton Fire Department is a modern professional organization staffed by thirty-five highly trained employees, fully equipped to handle emergencies—whether at a residence or at a high-rise in the downtown business district. The department moved into a new facility next to City Hall in 2004. The station houses a one hundred-foot quint (a truck with an aerial ladder, ground ladders, hose, and fire pump), a 1,500 GPM pumper, plus two ambulances, a command vehicle, and two staff cars. Since the purchase of its first ambulance in 1932, the Clayton Fire Department has also been on the forefront of emergency medical services. The department created the post of fire marshal in 1955 to emphasize fire prevention programs.

Clayton began taking steps to provide its own law enforcement soon after incorporation when Mayor Broadhead appointed J. H. Wengler to serve as city marshal until the election of April 1914. The first elected marshal—John Roth—resigned after four months of enforcing new city ordinances that required permits for animals and autos. The post paid one dollar a year, plus fees he collected from violators.

In 1920, the Board of Aldermen replaced the marshal system and ten board members became members of the new Clayton Police Department, which also had one full-time police officer. According to Dickson Terry, the city's officer continued to be paid a combination of salary and fees until 1930 when the Board of Aldermen set the salary at $150 month.

One hundred years later, the Clayton Police Department has a highly trained staff of fifty-two commissioned officers and fourteen civilian employees. The department is accredited by the Commission on Accreditation for Law Enforcement Agencies and is recognized as a leader among municipal police agencies in St. Louis County.

A $1.1 million solar project helps power the police department's new home—the landmark Heritage Building at 10 South Brentwood Boulevard. The city bought the Colonial Williamsburg–style building in 2009; the department had been headquartered at 227 South Central Avenue since 1962. After extensive renovations, the new headquarters is environmentally LEED Silver Certified.

Through the Years: Moments and Mayors

KEY DATES IN CLAYTON'S MUNICIPAL HISTORY

1912

December 18: Amid rumors that University City plans to annex part of their community, Clayton residents meet to discuss incorporation.

1913

January 27: Clayton citizens file an incorporation petition with the St. Louis County Court. According to the *Watchman-Advocate*, the plat for the new city reads as follows: *"Beginning on the west side of Coleman avenue at the Rock Island Railroad tracks, thence north to the north line of North Bemiston, thence east to the University City limits, thence south to the alley line in the rear of Hampton avenue, thence east to the east line of Jackson avenue, thence south to the south line of the Rock Island right-of-way, and thence west along the said right-of-way to the place of beginning."*

April 7: The county court grants Clayton's petition to incorporate. William F. Broadhead is appointed mayor. Aldermen are J.E. Dosenbach, F. J. Hollocher, Lee Barton, David Schmid, Oliver Jacobsmeyer, Harry Organ, Christ Ruehl, and George Wiedhahn.

April 16: At its first meeting, the city council sets boundaries for four wards and authorizes the appointment of a city clerk, city attorney, city assessor, treasurer, street commissioner, and night watchman. The number of wards would change several times in the city's early years. In October 1913, aldermen established six wards, but those were eventually reduced to five. The city of Clayton presently has three wards.

1915

May 12: Mayor Broadhead dies while on a fishing trip.

June 22: Fred L. Kerth becomes mayor after a special election. Kerth, who helped lead Clayton's incorporation crusade, will see the city through the World War I years.

1922

Julius R. Nolte is elected mayor. He continues necessary municipal improvements—sidewalks, curbs, and gutters—and forms the city's first planning commission.

1924

Roy P. Atwood, president of the Atwood Hay and Grain Co., is elected mayor and pushes for city improvements, including a new firehouse and the beautification of the old city park—then being used as a dump—behind the county courthouse.

1928

Edwin F. Stockho, a director and manager of the Lammert Furniture Co., is elected mayor. Stockho is instrumental in organizing the Clayton Relief Committee to aid needy families during the Great Depression.

November 4: Voters defeat a constitutional amendment to consolidate St. Louis County and St. Louis City. The "Save St. Louis County League" accuses the city of wanting the county's taxable wealth, while reminding voters that when the city and county split in 1876, "it left the county destitute—without a courthouse or the land on which to build one."

1929

December 23: Clayton passes an ordinance limiting smoke emissions from residences, factories, furnaces, and even steam locomotives to prevent the type of "blackouts" that regularly darken the skies over the city of St. Louis.

1931

July 2: Residents gather to dedicate Clayton's new city hall with an evening of speeches followed by dancing. The "Program of Dedication" notes that until the construction of this public building, the city government had met in "borrowed rooms" at the old

courthouse and above the Forsyth Engine House. Among the evening's special guests is Mrs. W. W. Henderson, the granddaughter of Ralph Clayton.

1932

December 23: Mayor Stockho dies of a heart attack.

1933

Charles A. Shaw is elected mayor, defeating Acting Mayor Jules Strong who had been appointed after Stockho's death. Shaw, a real estate executive, pledges efficiency in city government and will guide the city through the Great Depression. In 1937, the city's new Shaw Park is named for the mayor who acquired the land and the federal funds to develop it.

1940

Alfred H. Kerth, an attorney and nephew of Clayton's second mayor, is elected mayor. Kerth works to promote better relations with St. Louis City and County officials. After World War II, he organizes an effort to build temporary housing—Quonset huts—on the corner of Maryland and Gay avenues for returning veterans and their families.

1946

C. Kenneth Thies is elected mayor at a crucial moment in Clayton's development: a postwar retail boom fueled by the opening of a suburban Famous-Barr store in 1948.

1952

Roy A. Campbell becomes mayor, as commercial development continues at a whirlwind pace. Campbell must navigate a growing divide between residents and proponents of development.

1954

Jules A. Schweig is elected mayor, and the city considers changing its form of government to meet the challenges of rapid commercial development. Schweig presents an interesting report detailing twenty years of progress in the city. From 1934 to 1955, the city's assets grew from $372,297 to $1.97 million, and both the fire and police departments doubled their staffs.

1957

February 14: In a special election, voters approve a new charter that establishes a council-manager government. In July, Clifford W. O'Key is appointed as Clayton's first city manager.

1958

September 2: Mayor Schweig issues a progress report on the new form of government and pronounces it successful.

1959

F. William Human Jr. is elected mayor. During his administration, he and the Board of Aldermen are honored by the St. Louis Civil Liberties Commission for their work to integrate Clayton's restaurants.

April 14: Clayton's Board of Aldermen approves a new master plan for development that addresses traffic and parking issues and opens the door to high-rise buildings.

1963

Mayor William J. Hedley takes office, promising to uphold the city's development plans. He helps pass an ordinance requiring that future electrical wiring be placed underground to avoid visual pollution.

1967

Hy Waltuch is elected mayor. In 1969, he and the Board of Aldermen stir public controversy by proposing a half-cent sales tax. During Waltuch's term, the city purchases the Hanley House.

1971

After his election as mayor, James C. Laflin emphasizes city beautification and efforts to create a park in the DeMun area. He tells the *St. Louis Post-Dispatch*, "Compromise is my forte" and invites small groups of citizens to his office for coffee and discussion.

1979

J. Hunt Benoist, a construction executive, is elected mayor. Known for his community service, Benoist's company Hercules Construction built and remodeled various buildings in and around Clayton, including the Ritz-Carlton.

1983

Richard T. Stith Jr. is elected mayor.

1987

Former alderman Hugh Scott III becomes the new mayor. He brings a regional perspective to the post, having served as vice chairman of the St. Louis Regional Chamber and Growth Association.

1992

Attorney Benjamin Uchitelle is elected mayor after six years as an alderman. A former chairman of the MetroLink Commission, he emphasizes progress, education, and the arts.

1998

Francis L. Kenney III, an attorney and alderman for six years, is elected mayor. In his campaign, Kenney stresses the importance of working with other government agencies to enhance the infrastructure and environment of Clayton.

2004

Mayor Uchitelle is re-elected. In 2006, he signs the U.S.

Mayors Climate Protection Agreement, pledging to take action to reduce greenhouse gas pollution and prevent climate change.

2007

After serving eight years as an alderwoman, Linda Goldstein is elected as mayor, the first woman to hold the post. Goldstein, who was named one of the region's most influential people by the *St. Louis Business Journal*, has adopted a forward-thinking approach to environmental sustainability.

2010

The mayor and Board of Aldermen adopt Vision 2013, a plan to maintain Clayton's status as a preeminent regional business center and as a leader in environmental initiatives.

(Sources: Clayton city reports; *Watchman-Advocate*; *St. Louis Post-Dispatch*; *Clayton: a history* by Dickson Terry)

Chapter Two

City of Trees:
Residents are drawn to Clayton's clean air and rolling hills

"Where at night I hear whippoorwills and katydids . . . I think of the back porch and the luxurious Missouri sky before and under which I spent the most happy moments of my life."

—Clem Yore, writing to his Aunt Nancy Caroline Hanley, May 2, 1894

The Historic Hanley House, the oldest building in Clayton, has survived without major changes since it was built in 1855.

From the back porch of the Historic Hanley House, visitors today can glimpse the tips of skyscrapers in the Clayton sky. The city's present touches its past at this rose-pink brick farmhouse that was built more than a century and a half ago by Martin Franklin and Cyrene Hanley on their one hundred-acre farm. The house has been carefully restored and is now a city-owned museum, tucked away in a quiet one-acre park within walking distance of the downtown business district and its modern office towers.

Built in the Greek Revival style, the home speaks to the Southern ancestry of the Hanleys. Martin Franklin, who originally spelled his last name "Handley," was born in 1814 in Virginia. In 1847, he purchased land in St. Louis County near other Virginians who had also embraced the pioneer spirit and journeyed westward. Cyrene

Top left: Hanley family members gather on the farm in 1904.
Left: Hanley children Jim, Cal, Tom, and Net
Bottom: Hanley House, circa 1870

From *the* Headlines

Aunt Cal in her rocking chair

"AUNT CAL" TALKS TO THE PRESS

Nancy Caroline Hanley, the second of eleven children born to Martin Franklin and Cyrene Hanley, was a legendary figure in the Clayton community. She never married and lived in the Hanley House until she died in December 1938, just twenty-four days before her ninety-eighth birthday.

In an interview with the *St. Louis Post-Dispatch* published on June 3, 1934, Hanley, who was known as "Aunt Cal," recalled moving into the house after its construction in 1855. "When we moved in here our house was the only one for a considerable distance around and it commanded a splendid view over fields and woods toward St. Louis, which was then east of Grand avenue," she told the newspaper. "West of us were hundreds of acres of wooded land, most of which belonged to Mr. Clayton."

Nancy Caroline also talked about life in rural Missouri during the Civil War. The Hanleys were Southern sympathizers, as were many of their neighbors who were Virginia transplants. Nancy Caroline flew the Confederate flag from the porch of her home every year on June 3, the birthday of Confederate President Jefferson Davis. She told the *Post-Dispatch* of a morning, early on in the war, when seventy-five Union soldiers "invaded" the Hanley farm, while Confederate soldiers who were friends of the family hid in the nearby woods. Although her father initially refused to feed the soldiers, her mother intervened and breakfast was set out in the back of the house. Afterward, one of the Hanley girls played the piano while the others sang Southern songs.

"Meantime my sisters and I were busy trying to find a place to hide six Confederate shirts we had made for our boys," Nancy Caroline told the newspaper. "The only place we could think of was under our hoop skirts, and there the shirts stayed until after the soldiers left."

Clemens Walton was born in St. Louis County in 1819, but her parents—Judge James Walton and Isabella Musick Walton—both traced their roots to Virginia.

The Hanleys' two-story farmhouse was typical of homes constructed on Missouri farms in the mid-1800s. Its front and back porches accent its elegant practicality. Though the house has eight rooms, it was likely a tight fit for the Hanleys and the ten children they reared in it. Remarkably, the house is the only dwelling in existence from Clayton's earliest years. It was built in 1855—twenty-

PROFILE
THE HANLEY FAMILY

Once called "Hampton Hill" by Nancy Caroline Hanley, the old Hanley farmstead holds the memories of some of Clayton's earliest settlers. From photographs to letters, postcards, journals, and even marriage certificates, the treasures inside the museum paint a portrait of a loving, farming family. The ten children of Martin Franklin and Cyrene Hanley always called it home but once grown and married, their lives took many of them away from St. Louis County. Always fond of their country upbringing, the next generation of Hanleys frequently returned to Clayton to visit their Aunt Cal and Grandma Hanley.

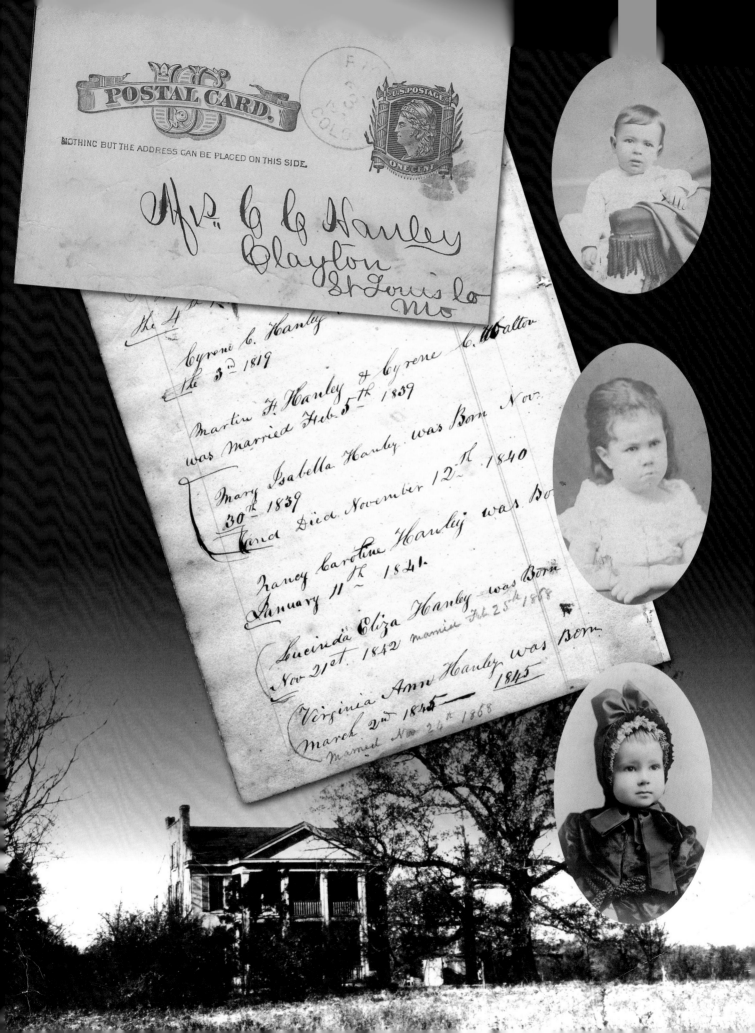

POSTAL CARD.

NOTHING BUT THE ADDRESS CAN BE PLACED ON THIS SIDE.

U.S. POSTAGE ONE CENT

Mrs C C Hanley
Clayton
St Louis Co
Mo

the 4

Cyrene C. Hanley
the 3rd 1819

Martin F. Hanley & Cyrene C. Walton
was married Feb 5th 1839

Mary Isabella Hanley was Born Nov.
30th 1839 and Died November 12th 1840

Nancy Caroline Hanley was Born
January 11th 1841.

Lucinda Eliza Hanley was Born
Nov 21st 1842 married Feb 25th 1868

Virginia Ann Hanley was Born
March 2nd 1845 1845
married Nov 24th 1868

two years before the Hanleys donated four acres of land to the effort to create a new county seat—fifty-eight years before Clayton incorporated.

The structure stands as a reminder of the community's rural heritage. According to Dickson Terry in *Clayton: a history*, early residents of the new county seat raised their own vegetables and also kept cows, chickens, and pigs. The town had dirt streets and plank sidewalks, and the nearest public transportation was two miles away.

Adele Starbird, a longtime columnist for the *St. Louis Post-Dispatch* and the dean of women at Washington University for twenty-eight years, recalled that the glory of Clayton at the turn of the twentieth century was found in its trees, not in the small frame houses and shops that had grown up around the St. Louis County Courthouse. Starbird, who was born in 1891, was the daughter of Henri Chomeau, the surveyor who laid out the county seat. Chomeau later built a home at the southwest corner of Meramec and Vena (now Westmoreland), where Starbird grew up.

Did you Know?

During the 1904 World's Fair, the present-day Wydown Terrace was the site of the Philippines Exhibit and the Igorot village attraction. The village was razed after the fair, and Hosmer Hall, a private girls' school, was built near the site. The School District of Clayton bought Hosmer Hall in 1936 and named it Wydown School. Early Wydown students used the name "Igorrote" for their yearbook and football team. In 2000, Wydown students invited American descendants of the Igorot tribe who had been exhibited at the World's Fair to participate in an educational and cultural exchange.

Although no fair buildings were moved to Clayton, residents did buy building material from structures disassembled after the exposition ended. While Forest Park was home to most of the exhibition, fair officials also leased the buildings constructed on the new Washington University campus. During the fair, Skinker Boulevard was named University Way and Forsyth Boulevard was Olympian Way.

Home of Harland Bartholomew (1889-1989), known as the Father of American and Canadian city planning.

Wydown Terrace neighborhood

From *the* Headlines

ALL ABOARD THE "04"

The first trolley pulled into Clayton on a Sunday in December 1895 loaded with ladies and gentlemen from the city of St. Louis enjoying an initial run before regular service started the next day, according to a report in the *Watchman*. After years of promises and false starts, streetcar service had finally arrived, courtesy of the Lindell Railway Company. It cost a nickel to ride the Forest Park and Clayton line from the county courthouse to Forsyth Junction at Union Boulevard in Forest Park. From there, another nickel bought passage on a Lindell Line car to Third Street and Washington Avenue in downtown St. Louis. The entire trip took about an hour.

The *St. Louis Post-Dispatch* also covered the beginning of operations of the "Clayton Electric Road," noting that the trolley would pass through a "fine suburban residence district" and that future development along the route was expected.

Clayton residents fondly referred to their trolley as the "Dinky" or "04," and for fifty years it toted them to work, school, and play. In later years, the trolley started its run in front of Washington University and then traveled along present-day Wydown Boulevard. The line eventually extended into western St. Louis County. In 1900, the St. Louis and Suburban Railway also started streetcar service to Clayton. That line ran from Kirkwood to Ferguson, passing along Pershing and Central avenues in Clayton. The Clayton 04 was shut down in 1947 and replaced by bus service. The Suburban Line discontinued service in 1963.

"The frame houses were of nondescript architecture, and landscaping consisted of red and yellow canna lilies, lilacs, flowering almond and syringa bushes were inadvertences," Starbird said in *Clayton: a history*. "But the glory of Clayton was its trees, mostly forest trees of hickory and oak. They made a bower of the Clayton of plank walks and dusty roads and white houses. Not a bad place to grow up."

During the nearly four decades that passed between the county seat's founding and incorporation, progress headed Clayton's way, driven by advances in transportation—trolleys and automobiles—that allowed city residents to seek country living in the woods and rolling hills of St. Louis County.

In 1895, the St. Louis Country Club opened on Hanley Road, the then southeast edge of Clayton, luring wealthy city residents to its impressive pillared clubhouse and sprawling land that had polo grounds, golf course, and stables. According to Dickson Terry, the club built its own road to the city limits, which

25

Chapter Two: City of Trees

Members of St. Louis Country Club pose with their dogs: from left, Erastus Wells, Harry Potter, Dan Catlin, Walter McKittrick, Harry Wallace, Oliver Richards, Ralph McKittrick, Eugene Pettus, George Simmons

Above: St. Louis Country Club, unknown year

Right: Country Club Court, unknown year

eventually became Wydown Boulevard. After a fire destroyed the country club in 1897, it was rebuilt and remained at the site until 1914, when members chose to relocate once again to wide-open spaces. By then, it was no longer out in the country but nearly in the heart of town. The site was subdivided and developed as Country Club Place; the polo grounds became the Polo neighborhood.

Top: Oak Knoll Rose Garden, view from the house

Right: Charles M. Rice's stone house in Oak Knoll Park is today the St. Louis Artists' Guild

Left: The dinosaurs at Oak Knoll Park moved to Forest Park after the Museum of Science and Natural History relocated as the Saint Louis Science Center to Oakland Avenue.

After the 1904 Louisiana Purchase Exposition, which had brought the world to nearby Forest Park, residential development continued to push toward Clayton from the western city limits of St. Louis. Dickson Terry credited W. L. Hemingway, president of the Mercantile Trust Company in St. Louis, for starting the migration of prominent St. Louis businessmen to Clayton. In 1905, Hemingway bought the Warfield home, a showcase at Hanley Road and Maryland Avenue that had been built in 1903 by E.W. Warfield, founder of St. Louis County Bank.

Shortly after Hemingway moved to Clayton, Charles M. Rice, a well-to-do St. Louis attorney, bought Oak Knoll, a large tract at Clayton Road and Big Bend (then Pennsylvania), and began to construct a magnificent stone residence. In 1910, the

THE NATIONAL REGISTER OF HISTORIC PLACES

Properties on the National Register have been recognized for their significance in history, architecture, engineering, or archaeology. This does not, however, guarantee their preservation. The owners of listed properties are eligible to receive federal tax credits and grant funds for restoration or rehabilitation purposes, but they still have the right to alter or demolish their properties as they choose (as long as no federal money is involved). If altered in such a way that affects its integrity, however, a property can lose its designation and be removed from the Register.

Listings in Clayton:

Brentmoor Park, Brentmoor, Forest Ridge Historic District

Big Bend and Wydown boulevards   *Listed: September 23, 1982*

Three private subdivisions plotted by architect and landscape designer Henry Wright, in the late nineteenth- and twentieth-century Revival style. Wright designed the homes to face inward, toward common grounds, in order to muffle the noise and congestion of the street and trolley. Residents included J. Lionberger Davis, Stratford Lee Morton, and Morton D. May.

Carrswold Historic District

1-26 Carrswold Drive, north of Wydown Boulevard   *Listed: September 9, 1982*

Private subdivision of twenty-three homes on thirty-five acres. Inset within the homes is a common ground designed by renowned landscape architect Jens Jensen, who favored using native flora. With the exception of four, the homes in Carrswold were built in the 1920s, primarily in the Tudor Revival style. Residents included Albert Keller, Oliver T. Peters, and Ella Lauman.

Haarstick-Whittemore Houses

6420 and 6440 Forsyth Boulevard   *Listed: September 20, 1982*

Henry Haarstick commissioned the homes, both built in 1912, for his daughters, Emma and Ida. In the mid-twentieth century, the family donated both homes to Washington University.

Hanley House, or Martin Franklin Hanley House

7600 Westmoreland Avenue   *Listed: May 27, 1971*

See narrative for the history of the house, page 20.

Hi-Pointe/DeMun Historic District

Roughly bounded by Clayton Road, DeMun Avenue,
San Bonita Avenue, and Big Bend Boulevard

Listed: May 7, 2005;
boundary increased March 22, 2007

Two residential subdivisions that share road and other architectural features. Architect and landscape designer Henry Wright plotted Hi-Pointe in 1917, and noted landscape architect Julius Pitzman laid out DeMun in 1923. Both subdivisions incorporate the natural topography of the land into their design.

Moorlands Additions Apartment District

Roughly bounded by Clayton Road, Glenridge Drive, Wydown Boulevard,
and both sides of Westwood Drive

Listed: September 30, 2009

Built in 1922 to be one of the county's elite private places. By 1925, focus shifted to an automobile-oriented district of apartment buildings. The buildings were primarily designed in the Tudor and Colonial Revivals, in keeping with the popular styles in Clayton, as well as the Art Deco and Modern designs.

Seven Gables Building

18-26 N. Meramec Avenue

Listed: July 16, 1985

Developed by Captain Gunter Meier and Norman Comfort with assistance of architect Daniel H. Mullen. The three-story stucco and brick Tudor Revival building was built in 1926 as a combination commercial-residential building.

Shanley Building

7800 Maryland Avenue, southwest corner of Bemiston Avenue
Listed: September 20, 1982

Designed by Harris Armstrong for orthodontist Dr. Leo M. Shanley in 1935. The building is the first example of the International style in this part of the country, using projecting and receding elements, as well as blocks of concrete glass. Armstrong won a silver medal at the Paris Exposition of 1937 for this design.

Wydown-Forsyth Historic District

Roughly bounded by Forsyth, Skinker, Fauquier and Wydown
Terrace, and University Lane
Listed: May 23, 1988

Residential neighborhood of 189 homes, 6 places of worship, and one school. It was designed to complement nearby Washington University. The majority of the homes were built between 1909 and 1941 in the Georgian or Colonial Revival and the Tudor Revival style. Architect James P. Jamieson designed many of the early Georgian and Tudor Revival homes.

Shanley Building

Henry Wright Park

Henry Wright
1878-1936

A renowned landscape architect and community planner, Wright designed three National Landmark cities and founded the post WWI New Town Movement. HiPointe was his first creation using New Town principles. The subdivision offers a range of housing options and businesses in a park-like setting. HiPointe is listed on the National Register of Historic Places as a nationally significant historic district (May 2005).

Names to *Know*

Among the noted architects and landscape artists working in Clayton during the early decades of the twentieth century were:

Henry Wright (Brentmoor, Brentmoor Park, Forest Ridge, DeMun Park, Hi-Point/DeMun). Wright, a major proponent of the garden city concept, assisted George Kessler, the lead landscape architect for the 1904 World's Fair.

Prussian-born city planner **Julius Pitzman** (The Moorlands, Claverach Park). Pitzman helped design Forest Park.

Jens Jensen (Carrswold). Jensen designed private estates and parks throughout the Midwest, including Columbus Park in Chicago.

Brent Tract Realty Company established Brentmoor Park, the first private and exclusive subdivision in Clayton, on thirty-four acres purchased from the estate of Alfred and Mary Young. James P. Jamieson, who designed the first buildings at Washington University, also designed some of the first homes in Brentmoor.

By the time Clayton incorporated, Forest Ridge, Skinker Heights, and Hillcrest were also in development. But civic progress had been slow going in the county seat, which depended on county funds for improvements. An ordinance approved on April 28, 1913, suggests that Mayor William F. Broadhead and the aldermen were determined to tidy up the rough edges of their new town. While most of their

Brentmoor Park neighborhood

early work dealt with staffing and revenue, Ordinance 3 prohibited "the use of violent, offensive conduct, loud noises, profane language, assaulting, fighting." Those found guilty faced a fine of up to one hundred dollars. At the same meeting, the council outlawed "animal cruelty, making false fire alarms, and using firearms, gun powder, and nitroglycerine without the mayor's permission."

Two years after incorporation the *Watchman-Advocate* published a harsh criticism of the county seat's lack of progress "outside of a few private granitoid walks and a pocketful of electric lights." In a front-page article on March 5, 1915, the newspaper reiterated its call to clean up streets and vacant lots that were covered with rubbish and tin cans and suggested that prisoners at the county jail could be put to work in the park south of the county courthouse. The headline summed up the *Watchman*'s frustration: "Let the City Dads Give Us Our Just Reward."

Between 1920 and 1930, the population of Clayton tripled—to just under ten thousand. In the blink of a few decades, the county seat had transformed from a rural outpost to a preferred residential community for St. Louisans wanting to escape the grit and congestion of the big city.

Clayton's private subdivisions featured architecturally striking homes in beautiful natural settings and set a new tone for the city—a fact noted by the *St. Louis Star-*

Moorlands
neighborhood

Wydown Forest neighborhood

Southmoor neighborhood

Claverach Park neighborhood

Skinker Heights neighborhood

Brentmoor neighborhood

Carrswold neighborhood

Ellenwood neighborhood

Clayton Gardens neighborhood

Tuscany Park neighborhood

Times in a special section in 1937 devoted to the "prosperous state of affairs" of the young city. Shaw and Francis Inc.—Mayor Charles A. Shaw's real estate company— listed the advantages of living in Clayton in an advertisement for the new Clayton Gardens subdivision being developed on the city's northwest side:

* High elevation overlooking the surrounding territory.

* One block from streetcars, buses, and service cars. Two blocks from the county courthouse.

* Good public and parochial schools within walking distance. Churches and shopping facilities nearby.

* Clean, healthful air—No smoke. Protected by Clayton's anti-smoke ordinance.

* Twenty-minute drive to downtown St. Louis, via Forsyth Boulevard or Delmar Boulevard or Clayton Road and the New Express Highway.

The Clayton Gardens promotion included a slogan—"Live in Clayton the City of Homes"—and stressed family values: "Master David and his dog are going to live in Clayton Gardens . . . David will have the advantages of Clayton's high-ranking schools." Another plus: This development of medium-priced homes was adjacent

Claverach Park neighborhood

to the city's new Charles A. Shaw Park with its swimming pool, tennis courts, and field house. The park was named for the mayor who arranged the land deal and then acquired federal funds from the Works Progress Administration to improve the grounds and construct facilities.

Shaw, elected in 1933, was a successful real estate developer by trade who helped guide the city through the trying times of the Great Depression. His firm had developed various Clayton neighborhoods, including Lake Forest, The Moorlands, and Claverach Park. The *Star-Times* gave the forty-year-old Shaw his due, describing him as an "aggressive young mayor typical of the city's spirit."

The newspaper also pointed out how far the city had come since it "was little more than a wide place in the road with only two or three sidewalks made of boards that had a way of flying up when a pedestrian stepped on one end of a section of it." The newspaper noted the city's emphasis on good homes and schools: "One of the most interesting features of this new Clayton is that it makes no plea for industries. Factories have their uses, but other places are welcome to them. The owners of industry are enthusiastically received in Clayton, but not their smokestacks."

Voices

May you abate the speeders, the noisy automobiles, prohibit heavy hauling on private streets, permit heavy hauling on private streets, remove telephone and light poles, erect telephone and light poles, stop advertising men from handing out circulars to passing automobiles, kill the too numerous squirrels, protect the squirrels because they are not numerous enough, stop the garbage wagon passing our homes, secure more garbage wagons passing our homes, find a burying place for dead calves and bird dogs, abate the noisy tractors at 7 a.m., and the loud radio sets at night, get the cows and jackasses out of your neighbors' yards, catch all the stray dogs, see that 50 pounds of ice goes as far as it used to, stop the firemen from snow-balling, get the streets oiled in front of everybody's house, see that too much oil is not put in front of everybody's house, keep the street lights burning and sewer the entire town.

—Mayor Julius R. Nolte shares advice on the difficulties of the job with his successor Roy P. Atwood in 1924; from *Clayton: a history*

Carrswold guard house

CLAYTON'S NEIGHBORHOOD LEGACY TAKES SHAPE

1855

May 15: Martin Franklin Hanley begins building a two-story house on his one hundred-acre farm in St. Louis County. Hanley notes the date in his daybook, amid routine ledger entries about supplies, wages, and other farm business: "Billy commenced work digging the cellar."

1880

Attorney William F. Broadhead, who would serve as the city's first mayor, builds the first home in the newly platted county seat—a two-story frame residence on the southwest corner of what is now Maryland Avenue and Brentwood Boulevard.

1900

Washington University begins construction of five buildings on its new campus, located on a hilltop west of the city limits of St. Louis. The design is based on the medieval courtyards of Oxford and Cambridge colleges.

1909

Architect James P. Jamieson, who designed buildings on the Washington University campus, carries that style into the Wydown-Forsyth residential neighborhood just south of Washington University. Period homes constructed between 1909 and 1941 provide a compatible setting for the university. In 1988, the district is listed on the National Register of Historic Places.

Thomas K. Skinker begins developing the Skinker-Heights and Ellenwood subdivisions, and later Hillcrest.

1910

Henry Wright, an architect and landscape designer, begins platting Brentmoor Park. He would also design Forest Ridge in 1911 and Brentmoor in 1913. The three subdivisions are on the National Register of Historic Places.

1911

Now known as the Alumni House, the Ellenwood House is designed by James Jamieson and constructed as the private home of Robert S. Brookings, then president of the Washington University Board of Directors.

1912

Jamieson also designs and builds the Whittemore House on Forsyth Boulevard across from Washington University, for the daughter of Henry Haarstick of the Mississippi Valley Transportation Company. The home now serves as a Washington University conference center and a private club for faculty, staff, and friends. The home is on the National Register of Historic Places.

The Skinker-Francis House is built on Ellenwood in the Skinker-Heights subdivision by Thomas Keith Skinker, secretary-treasurer of the Forest Park Railway Company.

He is the son of prominent Clayton landowner Thomas Skinker. The home is later bought by David R. Francis, who served as mayor of St. Louis, governor of Missouri, president of the Louisiana Purchase Exposition, and ambassador to Russia during World War I.

David R. Francis

1913

August 5: The new city of Clayton extends its limits to include Boland's Farm, the Carr estate, Brentmoor, Southmoor, Forest Ridge, Hill Crest, and Skinker Heights. Voters unanimously approve the annexation in an election described by the *Watchman-Advocate* as one of the quietest in the county: "A pinochle game helped pass the time among the judges and clerks."

Arthur Lambert, cousin of aviation pioneer Albert Bond Lambert, builds the home on Forsyth now known as the Stix International House. The home is later purchased by Ernest Stix, an original incorporator of the Municipal Opera and a director of Washington University. His wife, Erma Kingsbacher Stix, was a cofounder of John Burroughs School and a president of the St. Louis Suffrage League. The structure now serves as the Washington University International Student Center.

1917

Planner Henry Wright, a proponent of the garden city movement, prepares the plat for the Hi-Pointe subdivision. The Hi-Pointe/DeMun Historic District, roughly bounded by Clayton Road, DeMun Avenue, San Bonita Avenue, and Big Bend Boulevard, is listed as a landmark on the National Register of Historic Places.

1921

Catharine Boland sells the remainder of the 230-acre Claverach estate to the Moorland Land Company. The next year, Julius Pitzman designs Moorlands Addition as a private neighborhood. In 1926, revisions allow for period-style, low-rise apartments in what is now the Moorlands Park Apartment District; in 2009, the district is added to the National Register of Historic Places. The eastern half of the development becomes the Claverach Park neighborhood.

Davis Place neighborhood

Wydown Terrace is developed, just within the eastern city limits of Clayton. The subdivision has the distinction of being built on the site of what had been the Philippine Exhibit during the 1904 World's Fair. (According to local legend and newspaper accounts of the day, residents of Clayton may have provided dogs that were consumed by members of the Igorot tribe during the exhibition. A small lake in the exhibit is filled in with debris after the fair and becomes a park.) In 1993, the neighborhood is listed separately on the National Register of Historic Places.

1922

A group of St. Louis businessmen acquire the former country estate of Robert E. Carr, a prominent landowner who died in 1901. They retain noted landscape artist Jens Jensen to design a development known as Carrswold, now on the National Register of Historic Places.

1925

Davis Place is developed, the first private development in Clayton to allow both single and duplex family buildings.

1965

April: The Old Town Clayton Neighborhood Association meets to address concerns that the city is failing to respond to issues created by the overflow of commuters and shoppers from the downtown business district. Residents pull together, demanding development policies that will protect their neighborhood from traffic issues and real estate speculators. Members are the first to call for the preservation of the Hanley House as a historic place.

Mayor Hy Waltuch accepts deed to Hanley House, 1968

Chapter Three

Onward and Upward: Clayton grows tall as a regional hub of commerce

The auction of three hundred lots surrounding the St. Louis County Courthouse on June 6, 1878, didn't spark a land rush to the county seat, despite the pretty portrait painted by real estate agent Farrar and Co. in the sale announcement. All lots were fronted on wide streets and were "covered with a beautiful growth of forest shade trees. This property is in full view of the city of St. Louis and only six miles from Grand Avenue and two miles from Forest Park." Translation: The lots hadn't been cleared of trees and underbrush, and St. Louis wasn't that far away.

As would be expected, most of Clayton's businesses at the approach of the twentieth century were clustered around the courthouse. In 1948, Friederika Rauchenstein, widow of the *Watchman-Advocate* publisher, described this "district" in a letter to her great-grandson:

> *North of the* Watchman, *at the corner of Meramec and Forsyth, was the St. Louis County bank, started in 1889. The bank was about twenty-five feet wide, and David Schmid was the only teller. They had a large round safe in there. We called it the "Cannon Ball," and it was a great showpiece. On the north side of Forsyth, opposite the Court House, there were two or three saloons, and places to eat, and to sleep; also a grocery and the first bakery. . . . Then we had a butcher,*

BY THE
NUMBERS

$30,000 — Value set on Ralph Clayton's one hundred-acre donation to establish a county seat in 1878 (about $676,000 in today's dollars).

$300 — Value per acre of Clayton's donation in 1878 (about $6,760 per acre today).

$10 — Approximate price per acre paid by Clayton to John McKnight for his farmland in 1821 (about $199 per acre today).

$8 — Approximate price per acre paid for the ground in 1816 by McKnight. He bought the land from merchant Charles Gratiot who was granted 740 "arpents" of land—about 629 acres—in 1803 by the Spanish governor in what was then the Louisiana Territory (about $128 per acre today).

$6-$7 — Price per front foot for the lots surrounding the St. Louis County Courthouse square sold at auction in 1878 (about $135 to $158 per front foot today). Lots on other streets brought $2 and $3 per front foot (about $45 to $67 per front foot today).

Source: Historical sketch of Clayton written by McCune Gill, president of the Title Insurance Corporation of St. Louis

Sanguinet, and H.P. Wolff, who was first a butcher, and then opened a small grocery store at the northwest corner of Meramec and Carondelet. If one went there and asked for a dollar's worth of sugar, he would say, "I'll give you twenty-five cents worth, so I will still have some for another customer."

One hundred years after incorporation, Clayton's downtown business district still surrounds St. Louis County government buildings. The ten-story Government Center and six-story Courts Building were dedicated in 1970–71, and the district is still contained mostly within the boundaries of Ralph Clayton's one hundred-acre gift. The little wooden frame homes and shops are gone, however, and most of today's business dealings are conducted in glass and steel structures that reach for the sky.

Among the first high-rises to sprout in the business district was the sixteen-story Pierre Laclede Building on Forsyth, with the elegant Saint Louis Club on its top three floors, dedicated in 1964. The newest high-rise opened in June 2010: the seventeen-story Centene Plaza office tower at the corner of Forsyth and Hanley. The tallest—the thirty-floor Plaza in Clayton—is a residential tower completed in 2002.

Right: Pierre Laclede Building groundbreaking, 1962

Below: Pierre Laclede Building construction

The Clayton Famous-Barr, built in 1948, spurred a retail development boom.

Clayton's skyward climb started at street level in the 1940s with a retail boom. Suburban shoppers wanting to avoid traffic and lengthy commutes to downtown St. Louis shifted to retail shops in the county. The decision by May Department Stores to build its first suburban Famous-Barr store in Clayton encouraged additional development and led to a building spree of office buildings, according to research done in 1968 by Earl W. Kersten Jr. of the University of Nevada and D. Reid Ross of the St. Louis Regional Industrial Development Corporation.

They also pointed to Brown Shoe Company's move in the early 1950s from the wholesale district in St. Louis to a ten-acre tract on Clayton's Maryland Avenue. That relocation had "a strong psychological impact on the local business world," the researchers found, and Brown's move showed that a suburban location might be acceptable to large St. Louis companies. Their report, *Clayton: A New Metropolitan Focus in the St. Louis Area*, cited two major reasons that businesses were choosing Clayton: It was a desirable location providing easy access and relief from the congestion of downtown St. Louis, and it offered an atmosphere of growth and prestige with its modern buildings and attractive suburban landscape of homes, apartments, parks, and tree-lined streets.

In 1965, the Clayton Chamber of Commerce published a report titled *Mid-America's New Executive City*. The publication opened to an aerial view of the city's skyline and these words: "An unmatched American city with neither manufacturing nor slums, Clayton has maintained its residential integrity while undergoing a dramatic transition into the second downtown business district of Metropolitan St. Louis."

The chamber noted that controlled growth and planned development had enticed the highest caliber of businesses; nearly one hundred of America's five hundred largest corporations had offices in Clayton. Those offices represented all manner of business and marketing, from banking and law to the production of oil, steel, chemicals, automobiles, and textiles. Though, as the publication noted, "None of these things are made in Clayton. Probably no manufacture of consequence has existed here since Ralph Clayton set his workers to making shoes for a brisk covered wagon trade in the mid-19th century."

Such rapid progress rarely occurs without some push and pull between residents and developers, and one of the first visible protests occurred in 1953 when residents of Clayton Gardens picketed against rezoning along Maryland

Buster Brown and his dog Tige in an advertisement for Brown Shoe, 1903.

St. Louis County
Hospital, date unknown

Voices

Lee Evett, who served as city manager for fifteen years, said he was struck by the relationship between Clayton's neighborhoods and the business district when he arrived for his first job interview in 1976:

We stayed at the Colony Motor Hotel (now the Sheraton Clayton Plaza). We arrived in the middle of the hustle bustle of the downtown business district at 4 o'clock on a Friday afternoon. We went upstairs, unpacked, had dinner and then decided to walk around town. We walked out the front door and the streets were empty. Vacant. Nobody there. I'm thinking, "Was there a nuclear war and nobody told us? Is there an evacuation?" And then I saw two kids up the street with towels over their shoulders walking to the city swimming pool. We asked somebody about it, and he said, "It's after 5. Everybody's gone home." The community had taken over the business district. It literally transformed itself from one to the other just like that. I've never seen that before or since.

Colony Motor Hotel

Avenue to accommodate the American Investment Company office building. Such concerns prompted the city to begin developing a master plan to address the transition under way in the downtown business district: older houses and small shops giving way to tall modern office structures. The plan was adopted in 1959.

Clifford James, who served as Clayton's second city manager from 1965 to 1976, believes the master plan encouraged development in the business district—think of it as privately funded urban renewal—but also kept it from proceeding in a hodgepodge fashion. "The master plan, in effect, increased the value of the land, which was a win for the residents, and it also encouraged commercial development, so it was a win for the developers," James says. "The master plan also provided transition zones all around the downtown business district to make sure the business activity did not affect the surrounding neighborhoods. The master plan and the city council always took into consideration the residents first. I think that was the key. You just can't set twenty-four-story buildings next to houses."

The master plan also replaced old height restrictions with a ratio of open space to height: The more open space on the ground, the taller the building could be. In addition, all buildings were required to be set back at least ten feet from sidewalks.

Scruggs, Vandervoot & Barney advertisement
(right); intersection of Hanley and Forsyth (below)

Did you *Know?*

Clayton has seven million square feet of office space located in the downtown business district. Eighty-one percent of the city's 1,648 acres is devoted to residences and parks. The estimated actual value of Clayton real estate is about $2.7 billion (2012).

Douglas E. Geldbach, who headed Clayton's planning department for thirty-four years, started with the city shortly after the new zoning was approved. "Clayton has had other advantages, but the adequate planning and rigid adherence to the basic principles of the master plan are responsible for the high quality community that exists today," Geldbach concluded in an unpublished history he compiled about Clayton zoning. He also credited city leaders for continuing to adapt the master plan to meet changing situations.

THEN and NOW

The intersection of Brentwood and Forsyth boulevards, early 1960s

The interior streets of the new St. Louis County seat were originally named for the county and its townships: St. Louis, Central, Meramec, St. Ferdinand, Carondelet, and Bonhomme. Exterior streets were named for the county commissioners: William W. Henderson, Thomas J. Sappington, and Robert G. Coleman.

* Sappington is now Shaw Park Drive.

* Coleman later became North and South Road, and Brentwood Boulevard within the city limits.

* St. Ferdinand is now Forsyth Boulevard, named for Thomas and Robert Forsyth, early Clayton businessmen who owned land east of Clayton.

* Henderson became Maryland Avenue, after the street by that name was extended into the county. It was named for Peter and Jesse Lindell, prominent St. Louis merchants who were originally from the state of Maryland.

* St. Louis is Bemiston, for manufacturer Judson M. Bemis.

* Valley Avenue was changed to Pershing Avenue to honor General John J. Pershing, a Missourian who led the American Expeditionary Force in World War I.

Through the Years: Growing a Skyline

SOME KEY DATES IN CLAYTON COMMERCE

1887

The St. Louis, Kansas City and Colorado Railway, forerunner to the Rock Island Railroad, announces that it will begin stopping in Clayton, though the promised service is sporadic.

1890

The St. Louis County National Bank is established; it is the first bank in the county.

1895

The Olive Branch Electric Light, Heat and Power Co. provides the first electricity to Clayton.

The Lindell Railway Company begins streetcar service between Clayton and downtown St. Louis.

1901

The Kinloch Telephone Company brings telephone service to the county courthouse and the town of Clayton. Bell Telephone arrives in 1905.

1902

The forerunner of First National Bank of St. Louis is organized as the Trust Company of St. Louis County at 52 South Central in Clayton. One of the bank's first investments is a $4,500 bond to finance construction of a fence around the site of the 1904 World's Fair.

1913

The post office announces free home mail delivery for Clayton residents who put numbers on their houses and provide suitable receptacles for carriers to deposit the mail.

1914

Clayton residents agree to a ten-year contract with the Electric Company of Missouri to install streetlights.

1915

A new "jitney" service begins running between Clayton and St. Louis. The "big yellow seven-passenger Interstate automobile" can make the trip in less than fifteen minutes, reports the *Watchman-Advocate*.

1927

The Clayton Business Association is formed to boost the town and its advantages as a shopping center; the organization dissolves during the Great Depression.

1929

The city adopts its first zoning ordinance, prepared by planning firm Bartholomew and Associates. With an eye to the future, the code allows a building height restriction of 10 stories and 125 feet in height, though no high-rises are built at that time. The ordinance is amended 26 times between its passage and 1944, when it is replaced.

1931

The two hundred-bed St. Louis County Hospital opens on Brentwood Boulevard, following voter approval of a 1927 bond issue. Inpatient care is discontinued in 1986.

1935

Architect Harris Armstrong designs a distinctive office for Clayton dentist Dr. Leo Shanley. The structure at 7800 Maryland Avenue is an early example of the International style of architecture; it is listed on the National Register of Historic Places.

1941

Florist Byron Cade moves to Clayton Road. Later in the decade, they expanded the business to include gift merchandise and fine china.

Exclusive pottery arrangements of Spring flowers radiant with color for HER room.

Byron Cade
Flowers

Clayton at De Mun • CAbany 4701
ST. LOUIS, MISSOURI

1944

The city adopts a new zoning ordinance; buildings in the downtown business district are limited to three stories in height; multi-family building zones will serve as buffers between the commercial district and single-family residential areas.

1948

May Department Stores opens a 270,000-square-foot Famous-Barr store at Forsyth and Jackson.

A group called the Clayton Business and Professional Associates organizes to tackle the city's parking problems.

1950

The city issues permits for Scruggs, Vandervoort & Barney, Klines, and Garlands, within three blocks of Famous-Barr.

Work is completed on a new St. Louis County Courthouse.

1952

The city rezones the downtown business district, eliminating light industrial zones and increases building height limits to five stories.

Brown Shoe Company moves to Clayton and becomes the first business headquarters to locate in the city. The lobby features a mural by Fred Conway, a student of German artist Max Beckmann.

The Clayton Chamber of Commerce forms to promote city businesses. The organization begins with fourteen members; by its fiftieth anniversary in 2002, membership reaches 450.

1957

First National Bank of Clayton—formerly the Trust Company of St. Louis County—opens the first drive-through facility in Clayton.

1959

The city approves a master plan for development that removes height restrictions on buildings and replaces them with a ratio system of height and open space. New buildings must be set back ten feet from the sidewalk line to maintain a feel of openness.

1960

The city establishes an architectural review board.

1963

The sixteen-story Pierre Laclede Building, 7733 Forsyth Boulevard, is developed by Gregory J. Nooney, at a cost of about $7.5 million. The dedication in February 1964 features Madame Jean-Louise Chaudruc—a descendant of Pierre Laclede, the founder of St. Louis—who travels from France to christen the building with a bottle of French wine. Among the tenants is the St. Louis Club on the top three floors. Nooney later adds a twenty-four-floor tower at the site, now known as the Pierre Laclede Center.

Bernard F. McMahon erects the thirteen-story 230 Building at 230 South Bemiston. The Top of the 230 dining room offers elegant dining and a panoramic view.

1965

The Nooney Corporation builds the Hanley Towers, the first of the high-rise apartment buildings along Hanley Road. It is later converted to condominiums.

1966

Paul Londe builds the twenty-four-story Park Tower apartment building on South Brentwood Boulevard.

1969

Bernard F. McMahon builds the twenty-four-story 7777 Building on Bonhomme Avenue. At 312 feet, it is the tallest building in Clayton at the time.

Defense contractor General Dynamics relocates its national headquarters to the Pierre Laclede Center; the company stays in Clayton for twenty years, until it is purchased by Textron Inc. in 1992.

1970

St. Louis County dedicates a new government administration building, and in 1971 a new county courts building.

1973

The eighteen-story Chromalloy Plaza building is completed at 120 South Central Avenue. It is now the PNC Bank Center.

1975

The city revises its master plan to safeguard the residential nature of the Old Town neighborhood; eight square blocks had been added to the business district since 1947.

1982

Graybar, a Fortune 500 company that traces its history to 1869, moves its corporate headquarters from New York to Clayton.

1986

The nineteen-story Interco Corporate Tower is completed at 101 South Hanley Road.

1990

The Ritz-Carlton enhances Clayton's downtown landscape.

1993

Enterprise Holdings breaks ground for its new corporate headquarters at 600 Corporate Drive. Jack Taylor, who founded the company in 1957, grew up in Clayton. He attended Taylor School and graduated from Clayton High School.

2001

Construction is completed on the fourteen-story Shaw Park Plaza on North Brentwood.

2002

The thirty-story Plaza in Clayton tower opens at 150 Carondelet Plaza.

2006

MetroLink, the region's light rail system, comes to Clayton. The Forest Park Parkway passenger station named Forsyth Station opens at the northeast corner of the business district and Clayton Station opens in the heart of the district.

2010

Working with consultants Sasaki Associates of Boston, Clayton updates its downtown master plan to provide for future development and improvements in the downtown business district.

The Centene Plaza Office Tower opens at 7700 Forsyth Boulevard. The seventeen-story glass structure designed by Hellmuth, Obata and Kassabaum cost $186 million to build and rents for $33 a square foot. The structure is the first multi-tenant office in the region to earn a Leadership in Energy and Environmental Design Gold rating from the U.S. Green Building Council.

Enterprise Holdings

Chapter Four

Memories: *Residents savor small-town living in a big-thinking city*

On the first Sunday in June 1913, members of the Clayton Limburger Club piled into two trucks with their wives and guests and drove to Crystal Lake Park for an outing. Former Sheriff John Grueninger and hotelier George Autenrieth were in charge, ensuring that the "edibles and drinkables" were done to a queen's taste, wrote the *Watchman-Advocate* in a light-hearted report. "Fishing tackle was unwound and then tangled up in the lake. The largest catch of the day was credited to Mike Eble and measured just umpty steen inches and weighed icklety ogo pounds."

A highlight was watching former Judge Fred. L. Kerth round up thirty goats for an exhibition of fancy roping by the wives of the Limburgers. Mrs. George Wiedhan, wife of Clayton's Fourth Ward alderman, also delivered a soul-stirring address on women's suffrage.

The Clayton men's club was known for an odorous membership requirement—the ability to eat in one sitting a pound of the smelly German cheese that was their namesake. The *St. Louis Post-Dispatch* dubbed them the "strongest" organization in town and published a front-page cartoon of their picnic in June 1910. "They are very exclusive affairs, these Limburger picnics," the newspaper noted, adding that Grueninger wore a clothespin on his nose as he chopped the pungent cheese. "None but members can have any of the Limburgers. But everybody gets a smell."

When they weren't invading the countryside for their lively annual picnics, the Limburgers met at the Autenrieth Hotel. Brothers George and Henry Autenrieth, whose father George started the family's hotel and saloon business in 1878, claimed credit for forming the club. Members included some of the biggest cheeses in the community—prominent businessmen, judges, and county officials—who were helping to build Clayton into a city.

The Clayton Limburger Club meets at the Autenrieth Hotel Rathskellar, 1912

PROFILE
THE AUTENRIETH HOTEL

In the early days, travelers quenched their thirsts and rested their weary bones at the Autenrieth Hotel, the only hotel in town. The savvy George Autenrieth, who moved to Clayton while the courthouse was still under construction, recognized that lawyers and residents traveling to the county seat by horse and wagon would need food and lodging. He opened a tavern with rooms for rent on the north side of Forsyth near Meramec Avenue. When he later replaced his two-story frame hotel with a three-story brick structure, the old building was recycled: Newspaperman Frank W. Rauchenstein bought it and moved it across the street, next to the shop where he printed the *Watchman*.

Autenrieth, a German immigrant, became a forceful leader in his new community. He helped organize construction of the city's first one-room school in 1880 and the formation of the first volunteer fire department in 1897, after a fire threatened the town. He also helped found the first bank in the county and worked to bring streetlights to town. His funeral in 1899 was attended by prominent citizens from across the county and city of St. Louis. When the hotel burned in January 1911, Autenrieth's descendants opted to rebuild on the same spot. The Autenrieth Hotel dynasty ended in 1924. With Prohibition cutting into their sales, the family sold the Clayton landmark to Joseph Parks, who renamed it the Claymo Hotel. After Parks died on a fishing trip in Canada, his brother Larry ran the establishment. The building was later remodeled to house a clothing store and office building. It is now owned by David G. Danforth and David K. Schlafly of Autenrieth Properties.

Much of Clayton's early social life revolved around its churches and schools. Women organized coffee clubs and mothers' circles. They often met in one another's homes and set aside Sunday afternoons to call on their neighbors. The Limburgers limited its membership to twenty men, according to historian William L. Thomas, but the town also had a Masonic Lodge and a Knights of Columbus chapter. The Irish-American Society drew members from across the county and held a huge banquet every year on St. Patrick's Day. The society's membership revealed more Teutonic names than Celtic, Thomas wrote in *History of St. Louis County,* adding, "A local Clayton bard says: They are Irish one day in the year and German all the rest."

One of the earliest organizations was the Saengerbund, a German singing society that first met in 1881 at the Mount Olive House. The group later built a two-story hall on Maryland Avenue, west of Meramec, where residents gathered for parties, dances, and theatrical performances. The Saengerbund eventually grew to occupy an entire block of Maryland for its various activities.

Social organizations might serve a lump of civic affairs with their afternoon teas and musical soirees. At a meeting of the Tuesday Literary Club in October 1912, for example, members invited architect Henry Wright to discuss preservation of the county's natural beauty during future development, according to the *Watchman-Advocate.* Surveyor Henri Chomeau then explained sewer problems, and Judge John McElhinney talked about issues affecting the still-unincorporated community. The presentations were followed by vocal and instrumental selections and light refreshments.

As Clayton grew and transportation improved, residents found it easier to partake of St. Louis's wider array of entertainment and social opportunities.

Did you Know?

William Howard Taft, then the Republican candidate for president, spoke at the St. Louis County Courthouse in October 1908.

Former President Theodore "Teddy" Roosevelt (pictured), Taft's predecessor, addressed a crowd of 10,000 at the courthouse in October 1910.

Names to Know

Eagleton

Williams

Price

Poet **T. S. Eliot** was the grandson of the Reverend William Greenleaf Eliot, co-founder of Washington University and founder of today's First Unitarian Church of St. Louis.

Actor **James Franciscus** was born in Clayton in 1934.

Senator **Thomas Eagleton** lived in Clayton and taught at Washington University after serving nearly two decades in the U.S. Senate.

Politician **Sam Goddard**, who served as governor of Arizona, was born in Clayton in 1919.

Actor **Kevin Kline**'s parents, Peggy and Robert Joseph Kline, opened a branch of Kline's Incorporated, their St. Louis women's apparel store, at 7620 Forsyth Boulevard in 1951. Kline's father also owned and ran the Record Bar, a well-known Clayton toy and record store on Brentwood Boulevard. The building later housed the first bookstore of The Library Ltd.

Artist **Ernest Trova** was born in Clayton in 1927 and attended Clayton High School.

Playwright **Tennessee Williams**, whose family lived in Clayton for a time, attended Washington University. In 1937, after his anti-war play *Me Vashya* placed fourth in a student competition, Williams "stormed into his professor's office before storming out of St. Louis altogether," according to Washington University's news service that wrote about the incident in December 2003. In February 2004, the university's performing arts department staged the play, which had been stored in the archives and never published.

Actor **Vincent Price**'s family home was on Forsyth Boulevard. Price, the master of the horror film, was the son of Marguerite and Vincent Price Sr., the president of the National Candy Company.

And there were also more options in their own backyard. In April 1915, Edward Tegethoff opened the first "Airdome" on Forsyth Boulevard, just east of Central, to begin showing "high-class" moving pictures. The *Watchman-Advocate* was thrilled, commenting, "No more will we have to inhale the smoke-filled atmosphere of a poolroom . . . or ride several miles on a street car to fill an evening with enjoyment."

In an oral history conducted in 1976 by students of Wydown Middle School, Polly Day recalled shopping at Gutman's Department Store on the corner of Forsyth and Meramec. The Gutman family sold dry goods at that location from 1901 to 1955 and had a barbershop for children. For Day, a visit to Gutman's was just a streetcar ride away:

A mother could send her children up to Gutman's on the 04. She would always know that once they got off at Gutman's, Mr. Gutman would make sure they got what they needed. After they were done with their shopping, he would see to it that they got back on the 04 for their return home.

55

Chapter Four: Memories

1913

Total population of Clayton: 1,948

White: 1,801

Black or African-American: 137

Japanese: 10

(Based on a census taken after incorporation by City Collector Henry Stecker, who noted that the ten Japanese residents were waiters at the St. Louis Country Club.)

2010

Total population of Clayton: 15,939

White: 12,432

Black or African-American: 1,306

Asian: 1,721

Other: 480

(Source: U.S. Census Bureau, 2010 American Community Survey, as reported on Claytonmo.gov.)

When asked about living in Clayton, longtime residents often focus on the small-town feel of their modern, urban city. While the high-rises that sprouted in the downtown business district in the second half of the century are impressive, residents are more likely to describe life at ground level: where they went to school, bought pastries, got their hair cut, or sipped a cola or a cocktail.

Former Senator John C. Danforth, who served nineteen years in the U.S. Senate, shared memories of growing up in Clayton with *St. Louis Magazine*, published in January 2012:

John C. Danforth

There was a drugstore at Forsyth, and we'd stop there and get a cherry Coke. I was in Harold Bauer's Standard station one time, right where Wydown runs into Hanley, and [Cardinals shortshop] Marty Marion drove in. Across the street was the Glaser Drugstore, I think it's a Starbucks now, so I went in and bought a Looney Tunes and Merrie Melodies comic book, and Marty Marion autographed my comic book. There was the bowling alley, Lee's Grill for hamburgers, Pevely Dairy for ice cream. Clayton was very different then, really a small town. The buildings were all two-story. There was a trolley, the Clayton 04. . . . You'd take the streetcar all over the place. Even for a child, there was not a sense of danger.

Voices: Race Relations

In 1976, students from Wydown Junior High School published *Images of Our Community—Clayton*, a remarkable booklet that delved into the history of their community. As part of their research, the students recorded interviews with Clayton residents on topics ranging from education and Clayton commerce to the importance of religion. In a notable chapter titled "Race Relations in Clayton," the students wondered why so few African-Americans live in the city and questioned longtime residents about race relations in the early days.

The young authors noted that most residents stressed the spirit of friendliness and respect between the races. Adele Starbird, a longtime columnist for the *St. Louis Post-Dispatch*, discussed the small African-American neighborhood southeast of the courthouse—and also provided a glimpse into a more conflicted point of view:

I remember that street where blacks lived very well because we didn't have any telephones when I was a child. If we wanted extra help or something, I was sent down there to see the Claibornes or to get Mollie to come up for some work. They all owned their own houses and they were well-painted nice little cottages there at Carondelet and Bonhomme. . . . My grandmother was a rather rabid pro-Southerner, but she was perfectly delighted to have me ride on the grocery wagon driven by Mr. Coleman (a black man). . . . But then they appointed a Negro postmaster in Clayton and after that nobody in our family—the women of our family—was allowed to go to the post office for a while. I would go down to my father's office, but I was not allowed to go to the post office. It was all right for me to be with Coleman, but not right for me to go to the post office. This distinction always amused me very much.

The students asked Bertha B. Rhoda, who taught summer classes at Clayton's Crispus Attucks School for African-American children, if she believed her students felt bothered or hurt by being segregated. Rhoda, an African-American, replied: "No, I don't feel that they did. They were just children and it was their school. Children do not see the things that adults see."

The Wydown students also interviewed Evelyn Johnson, who attended Attucks, which educated students through the eighth grade. She said:

I graduated from Attucks in 1946. . . . I understand that the Clayton Board of Education screened Miss Thomas (the teacher) very thoroughly. I think that she even had her master's degree. She wasn't someone that they had just selected and sent in to fill the void or the need of black students. . . . Rather than have us come to the [Clayton] high school, they paid our tuition to various schools. My family went to Sumner High School. There were some that went to Vashon. Others went to Douglas in Webster Groves. These were all black schools.

Asked about race relations in the community, Johnson told the students:

You didn't have to worry about someone being afraid to walk in the area because they were of another color. There were some whites that went out of their way to be nice and there were others who ignored you.

I think that the black families that were there were respected families. There was certainly an understanding between whites and blacks—it was certainly an acceptance. We didn't have house-to-house visits unless there was an illness. Very often whites came in to see if there was anything they could do.

Voices: Great Depression

There were no bread lines in Clayton during the Great Depression, but men and women did gather outside the local office of the Works Progress Administration (WPA) hoping to find work. Service organizations responded to the growing economic crisis in the early 1930s by staging benefits to help the jobless. In 1932, three thousand applicants signed up with the county's Free Employment Bureau, and Clayton Mayor Ed Stockho appointed a Citizens Relief Committee, headquartered at City Hall, to distribute food and clothing to the needy. In his history of Clayton, Dickson Terry wrote about a group of women who worked on behalf of children but asked the newspapers not to print their names:

In the winter of 1932-1933, a "Children's Kitchen" operated by some 60 women, was set up at 14 No. Meramec to provide lunches for about 500 school children in Clayton and the county whose parents had been hit by the depression. Daily lunches were sent out and served in the school cafeterias in such a way that they could not be distinguished from the lunches of those who were able to pay. The women solicited the food. Some would collect it, others cook it, and still others take it to the schools each day. The food was donated by merchants, dairies, bakeries and farmers.

Genevieve Neaf, who was born in 1922, recalled stories told by her father, who was elected as the first Democratic assessor in St. Louis County in 1932. Martin L. Neaf obtained federal grants and hired out-of-work engineers and college graduates to reassess the county:

One Christmas he came home with tears streaming down his cheeks. These people each had chipped in ten cents and bought him a fountain pen and pencil set. He said he felt he had taken a loaf of bread from each of their families.

On December 22, 1933, the *Watchman-Advocate* reported that St. Louis County's disbursing officer had signed thousands of paychecks, as Civil Works Administration (CWA) workers waited:

The long line of thinly clad men and women who stood for hours and hours in line—pinched by cold and hunger—awaiting their turn in being assigned to CWA projects was visible evidence of the widespread suffering and distress which gripped so many of our good citizens.

Off to work they went, and then came payday, a magic word in the dark days of depression: but while workers toiled with pick and shovel, with hammer and saw, and at all tasks, and even while they slept between days, there was one man in St. Louis County charged with the responsibility of signing the Government checks. Richard Chomeau, County Disbursing Officer, worked continuously from Friday morning until Saturday night—36 hours at a stretch—and signed 7,065 paychecks.

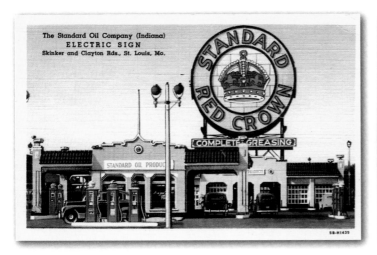

Clayton Road's landmark gas stations

The large downtown retailers that rushed to open suburban branches after World War II have moved on, but the city has attracted a new and diverse array of boutiques and specialty shops. The old Famous-Barr store, built to hug the curve of Forsyth Boulevard, is now owned by Washington University and houses Ivey-Selkirk Auctioneers and the Wine & Cheese Place, while another sweeping retail structure—at Forsyth and Maryland—is still home to Straub's grocery. The two-story structure with its signature circular stairwell remains a "most unusual food market," just as when it opened in 1948.

Today, old and new enterprises stand side by side in Clayton's neighborhood business districts. On Wydown Boulevard, a third generation of Protzel's is still serving the finest corned beef since 1954 in their compact deli. Next door at the sleek and ultramodern Chill, patrons top their own frozen yogurt. The streetcar tracks that once carried the Clayton 04 along Wydown have been lost to history, but in 2010 the American Planning Association named the redesigned boulevard one of "America's Great Streets" for achieving balance between planning and preservation.

Depot Dance, 1960s

PROFILE
GUTMAN'S

For the first half of the twentieth century, Gutman's store was *the* shopping destination for Clayton residents. Adolph Gutman, who first set up shop in Clayton in 1901, built the landmark store at the northwest corner of Forsyth Boulevard and Meramec Avenue. Gutman's not only sold a wide array of clothing and general merchandise, but the store also featured a barbershop for children. Adolph Gutman, pictured at top left with son Louis riding a donkey, was also active in Clayton civic affairs. Gutman's sons, Louis and David, carried on the business until the mid-1950s.

PROFILE
STRAUB'S

In 1948, William A. Straub, right, opened an air-conditioned "super-market" on the southwest corner of Forsyth Boulevard and Maryland Avenue. The store, designed by St. Louis architect Raymond E. Maritz to follow the curve of the street, boasted a delicatessen, a winding staircase to a second-floor restaurant and an ice cream–making facility in the basement. The *St. Louis Post-Dispatch* described the new market in a February 29, 1948, article as "the most extraordinary food dispensing establishment in the United States." For six decades, the store has "dispensed" fresh produce and fine meats, baked goods and specialty grocery items, including its "world-famous" chicken salad. The location also serves as corporate headquarters for Straub's Markets, still owned and operated by the Straub family.

In an essay written in 2002 for the Clayton High School alumni newsletter, Andy Rochman described life in the 1950s and his after-school visits to Wydown Shoe Repair that served Clayton residents for eighty years. Dominic Cerulo opened the shop in 1931, and his son Jack Cerulo carried on the business until 2011. Before visiting with the Cerulos, Rochman would stop at Glaser Drugstore (now a Starbucks) next door:

> At Glasers, we satisfied the U.S. RDA requirement for fats, salts, sugars and preservatives. For 55 cents, which included tax and tip, you got to sit at the soda fountain counter, swivel continuously on the back-breaking, round dark, green vinyl covered stools, and wolf down a handmade hamburger topped with a whale-thick slice of Bermuda onion, hot and greasy hand-cut French fries and a hand-mixed cherry Coke with those miniature crystal-clear ice cubes (they were actually little square tiles).

Yes, those were the days . . .

PROFILE
THE SEVEN GABLES INN

The Seven Gables Building, now a boutique hotel on North Meramec, was built in 1926 by real estate developers Gunther Meier and Norman Comfort. Architect Dan J. Mullen designed the structure in the Tudor style of English architecture to suit the tastes of Meier and Comfort. The building originally contained offices, several storefronts, and apartments aimed at attracting middle-class residents. Rent in 1927 was $57.50 a month for a three-room efficiency, according to an ad in the *St. Louis Globe-Democrat*. The Balke group renovated the building in 1986. It is now owned by St. Louis–based Lodging Hospitality Management, founded by Robert O'Loughlin. The Seven Gables is listed on the National Register of Historic Places.

BY THE NUMBERS

The price of lunch

17¢ – Sandwich at the Parkmoor, circa 1930

5¢ – A cherry Coke in 1930

$6 – A "calf burger" at the Fatted Calf in 2012

$1.50 – Price of a fountain drink today

Through the Years: Gathering Places

1882

The Saengerbund Society, a German singing group, holds its first festival. The society later builds a two-story hall on Maryland Avenue, west of Meramec, that becomes a center for social events. In 1905, the hall is converted into a church by the Samuel German Evangelical Church. It is torn down in the 1940s.

1895

The St. Louis Country Club relocates to the Clayton countryside, just south of town. In 1897, it burns to the ground in a spectacular fire. The club rebuilds and remains at the location until 1914.

1906

A band of wandering gypsies sets up camp near Washington University and applies to the Circuit Court in Clayton to incorporate as the National Gypsy Association of America. The group makes headlines in the area for several years before moving on.

1908

Dr. G. C. Eggers opens a two-story medical building on Central Avenue near the northeast corner of the courthouse square. It is the most "modern" building in town. His office is upstairs; a pharmacy and a small ice cream parlor are on the lower level. Ice cream sodas and sundaes cost a nickel.

1910

John O'Gorman opens a hardware store in the Oncken Building at what would become 28 North Central. After O'Gorman's death in 1921, Frank Human buys the inventory and reopens the store. In 1927,

Human Brothers Hardware moves to a new building at 30 North Central.

1912

The *Watchman-Advocate* opens a new office at 410 Central Avenue. The modern steam-heated building advertises that it will print anything from a calling card to a catalogue. "In politics it is Republican and has been fighting for the interests of the Grand Old Party," an ad says, "but it gives Democrats and all others a square deal."

1915

Edward Tegethoff opens an "Airdome" on Forsyth Boulevard, just east of Central, to begin showing "high-class" moving pictures; admission is ten cents.

1917

Three thousand people gather at the courthouse to honor fifty-two St. Louis County men leaving for duty in World War I. The men were headed to the Army's Camp Funston in Kansas. Nineteen of three hundred eligible Clayton men were selected in the first round of the draft.

1919

The Horn-Stecker post of the American Legion is established in Clayton and named for Leslie Horn and Joseph Stecker, two soldiers from Clayton who died during World War I. Horn, twenty-three, a second lieutenant in the 13th Infantry, was killed in the first battle of the Argonne; Stecker, twenty-seven, was a casualty of the Spanish Flu pandemic in 1918.

1921

George M. Khoury buys and remodels the Tegethoff Airdome, adding a stage for live performances. Khoury would later become famous for founding the Khoury League, a youth baseball league.

1924

The Clayton Rotary Club, one of the city's oldest civic organizations, is formed during a meeting of twenty-five prominent business and professional men at the Claymo Hotel.

1930

William McGinley opens the Parkmoor Restaurant on Clayton and Big Bend, the first drive-up restaurant in the St. Louis area. The restaurant evolves into a sit-down diner—a Clayton classic until it closes in 1999.

Parkmoor french fried Potatoes 12c

Parkmoor french fried Onions 17c

The Pevely Fountain opens on Forsyth. The dairy attracts loyal customers with its nickel ice cream and colorful fountain that shoots water thirty feet into the air.

1933

The 465-seat Shady Oak movie theater opens at the intersection of Forsyth and Hanley, previously the site of an outdoor theater shaded by an oak tree. Wehrenberg leases the single-screen theater in 1977 and keeps it open until August 2000.

William A. Straub, who has run a grocery in Webster Groves since 1901, opens a market in Clayton.

1934

The first Clayton library opens in a room of City Hall. Residents donate one thousand books to fill the shelves. Titles highest in demand in the spring of 1935 are *Goodbye, Mr. Chips* by James Hilton, *Now in November* by Josephine Winslow Johnson, and *So Red the Rose* by Stark Young, according to the *Watchman*. In 1937, the city receives a $35,000 grant from the Public Works Administration to build an addition to City Hall to house a larger library.

1958

Bernard F. McMahon builds the first hotel in Clayton since the closing of the old Autenrieth Hotel. The three-story Clayton Inn has forty-two rooms.

1960

Cyrano's opens at Clayton Road and DeMun Avenue and quickly becomes the place to go after the movies, theater, or prom for coffee and ice cream concoctions topped with towers of whipped cream. After a fire in 1979, the iconic evening spot moves to a location on South Big Bend Boulevard.

1969

The Fatted Calf chain, originated by Vince and Tony Bommarito, begins serving burgers at its new location on South Bemiston. Forty years later, the restaurant has new owners but still sells Calfburgers and fries.

1971

The Clayton library merges with the St. Louis County Library and is renamed the Mid-County branch. A new facility opens in 1977 at 7821 Maryland Avenue.

1976

The Rotary Club organizes the Clayton 1776 Fair to celebrate both the nation's bicentennial and the 1977 centennial of Clayton as the county seat. The event is held on July 3 and 4 at Shaw Park.

1983

The Clayton Chamber of Commerce begins holding "Parties in the Park" at Shaw Park. The popular outdoor after-work events feature live music, entertainment, and refreshments. In 2011, the summer series is renamed "Parties in the Park in Downtown Clayton" and moves to Meramec Avenue between Forsyth Boulevard and Maryland Avenue.

1992

After previous locations on Brentwood and Forsyth boulevards, Terry and Allen Mittelman open the third version of The Library Ltd. in the former Vandervoorts building at Hanley Road and Forsyth Boulevard. The children's section features a fourteen-foot castle with a goldfish-stocked moat. The bookstore hosts book signings every week, attracting such famous authors as Newt Gingrich, Colin Powell, Hillary Clinton, Martha Stewart, Gloria Steinem, and Frank McCourt. Borders buys the business in 1997. In 2008, the Centene Corporation demolishes the structure to make room for the company's new corporate headquarters.

1994

A new gathering spot—Kaldi's Coffeehouse—opens at the corner of DeMun and Northwood avenues in the DeMun historic area.

1963

The Mainlander, a quirky Polynesian restaurant and bar, opens at Bonhomme Avenue and Hanley Road, the former location of the Crispus Attucks School. In 1989, the seven-story Bonhomme Place building is erected on the site.

Shaw holds check for the library, 1934

Chapter *Five*

*L*earning in Clayton: "E" is for Excellence and "I" is for Innovation

On Saturday evening June 6, 1931, Clayton citizens flocked to attend the farewell assembly for Forsyth School. The school's bell rang for the last time, summoning teachers and students—both current and past—to say goodbye to Clayton's first brick school building, which had also served as the city's first high school. After thirty-nine years, Forsyth could no longer accommodate the growing population of the school district, and it was being replaced.

Festivities included displays of photographs, and addresses delivered by Superintendent John. L. Bracken and Marie Turner Harvey, the school's first principal. The time capsule from the building's cornerstone was opened, revealing copies of newspapers and compositions written by the school's first students. Afterward, friends gathered around the punch bowl and told stories of bygone years. For four decades, Forsyth had been a vital piece of the School District of Clayton, and its construction had marked an important step in the growth and progress of the city.

Public schools in Clayton trace their origin to March 5, 1880, when a group of citizens led by George Autenrieth gathered at the county courthouse to discuss opening a public school. At a town meeting on April 22, taxpayers voted to form the School District of Clayton, elect directors, and most importantly, build a schoolhouse. On June 15, the new district purchased a tract of land from the

Left: Today, the Forsyth School moniker is used by an acclaimed private elementary school on Wydown Boulevard.

Below: Forsyth School kindergarteners, 1928

county court and built a one-room frame structure. It cost $700 (about $15,400 in today's dollars) and took one month to build. Forty-eight students enrolled initially—forty-five white students and three African-American students.

Enrollment grew with the town, and by 1887, the school district had outgrown its one-room, one-teacher schoolhouse. An addition was constructed, and the school's staff added Turner as principal and a teacher at salaries of $60 a month (about $1,420 today). By 1890, the district's directors—George Autenrieth, Robert Shnecko, and Emil L. Dosenbach—decided

Did you Know?

Katherine M. Autenrieth, who was born on the day after Christmas in 1879, is believed to be the first person born in the newly platted county seat. Her father, hotelier George Autenrieth, initiated the effort to build the first school in the community.

Voices

Adele Starbird, a prominent Clayton resident who started at Forsyth School in 1898, recalled her teacher's emphasis on academic excellence in a 1976 interview with Wydown middle school students:

I remember the geometric blocks of beautiful wood we put together and played with in the primary grades—cylinders, pyramids, and spheroids. In the fourth grade we made costumes and stage props for a play, Hiawatha. *I still recall the lines. . . . Our teacher . . . took us out to do water colors in the lovely fields of wild flowers that surrounded the school. She also had us do 15-minute sketches in English and encouraged creative, free expression in so many ways. I still have that work and find it hard to believe that a teacher could get such work from fourth graders.*

In an essay submitted to the Clayton History Society's website, Gerry Schiller shared a parent's point of view:

If the DeMun area was magical for me as a child, Davis Place, and Meramec School was its counterpart for young married families with young children. It was a very social enclave, complete with school shows, conceived, directed by and performed by the parents of the Meramec classes . . . they were great fun and eagerly awaited . . . I remember specifically the parent meetings that were heavily attended to bring the schools into the world of Sputnik (the Russian science threat). . . .

that a new two-story building was needed to educate the youth of Clayton properly. Taxpayers approved funding to build a school on a one-acre site, to be purchased from St. Louis County.

This land, however, would not be acquired as easily as the directors expected. Martin Franklin and Cyrene Hanley had donated that parcel, along with three other acres, to the county in 1877. After her husband died in 1879, Cyrene continued to live in the Hanley House, near the donated land. After the sale, she refused to turn the property over to the school district. While it has been speculated that Hanley didn't want all of Clayton's schoolchildren so near to her home on a regular basis, she argued that the county had let too much time pass without acting upon the land. The school district filed suit against Hanley, and multiple court cases followed, but by April 1892, the two parties reached a compromise.

After resolving the conflict, the School District of Clayton voted to instead build two schools. The new schoolhouse on the Hanley land would house grades 1-8. The original school property would be sold and the revenue used to build a separate school for the African-American children of the area.

On October 21, 1892, Clayton dedicated Central or Clayton No. 1—later known as the Forsyth School. The two-story, eight-room building on Lee Avenue cost $17,000 to build. The front page of the *Watchman-Advocate* presented a detailed sketch of the school, an impressive building with tall windows and two symmetrical turret-like towers, presided over by a high-flying American flag.

The Crispus Attucks School for African-American children followed in 1894, located where the seven-story Bonhomme Place office building now stands. The Attucks School was a one-room frame building, much like Clayton's first public school. In 1921, voters in the district overwhelmingly passed a proposition

Top: Crispus Attucks School children, date unknown

Bottom: Crispus Attucks School, date unknown

Bellevue School, Class of 1958

Bellevue School, date unknown

to replace this school with a new brick building, at a cost of $16,000. That school, also called Crispus Attucks, was completed in 1923 at the same location.

After the turn of the century, it became evident that Clayton needed more than two schools. In 1906, Bellevue School, originally known as Clayton School No. 2, opened to serve students in the southeastern tip of Clayton. The school district also decided to begin providing a secondary education to Clayton's youths, who previously enrolled in the high schools of St. Louis. The second floor of Forsyth (Clayton No. 1)

Wally Lundt coaches a water polo class, date unknown

Clayton High School, Class of 1916

was converted into a high school, and additions were constructed to house grades 1-2. Clayton's new high school was segregated, and since there was no dedicated African-American high school in Clayton, the district paid for Attucks graduates to attend high schools in St. Louis.

Clayton's first senior class—five girls and four boys—graduated on June 16, 1911. The school celebrated with a night of "musical and literary numbers," in the words of the *Watchman-Advocate*. Dr. Frederick A. Hull, a professor at Washington University, delivered the address.

In 1913, Clayton High saw a 50 percent increase in enrollment, making it one of the fastest-growing schools in St. Louis County. The schools were filled to capacity, prompting discussions about building a freestanding high school. The first bond issue failed, but in April 1916,

Clayton, Missouri: An Urban Story

PROFILE
AND THE EARTH MOVED

The Clayton High School community gathered to dedicate its new Centennial Plaza on December 13, 2011, but before that could happen the earth had to move. In September, the Globe—the iconic ten-ton gray granite sculpture that has stood at the front entrance of the school since 1953—was moved to a pedestal in the new plaza. Construction workers used a heavy-duty crane to move the sculpture, which was designed by Lester C. Heckle and is the namesake of the high school's newspaper. The Centennial Plaza project, designed to serve as a gathering place for students and visitors, celebrates one hundred years of Clayton High School.

voters approved the construction of Clayton High School. It opened in 1917 with one hundred students in attendance. The three-story, twenty-eight-room building cost $125,000 (about $2.13 million today).

The fall of 1954 heralded great changes for the School District of Clayton. The Supreme Court ruling in *Brown v. Board of Education* declared that the "separate but equal" practice established by *Plessy v. Ferguson* fifty years earlier was unconstitutional. For Clayton, this meant that the students of Attucks School could no longer be segregated. The district worked swiftly to implement integration within its boundaries, a goal accomplished by opening day of the following academic year. In fall 1954, a full nine months before the *Brown II* ruling ordered schools to integrate with "all deliberate speed"—and fifteen years before the national legal mandate to do so—Clayton's white and African-American students studied together for the first time in the twentieth century. No longer needed by the district, the Attucks School was closed and demolished. It had served Clayton for thirty-one years.

That September, Clayton high school students met new classmates and moved into a new school building on Mark Twain Circle. In May 1955, Erwin France became the first African-American graduate of Clayton High. The 1955 CHS

Washington University

Washington University was founded in 1853 by Wayman Crow, a prominent St. Louis merchant, and his pastor, William Greenleaf Eliot Jr., who were concerned about the lack of institutions of higher education in the growing Midwest. By 1892, the university was operating out of six buildings on Seventeenth Street in St. Louis, and the city's growth threatened the school's existence. Robert Somers Brookings, a wealthy member of the board, sought a unified campus outside of the city. In 1893, he selected a hilltop location west of the city on 103 acres of open country and woods stretching from Skinker to Pennsylvania Avenue (now Big Bend). Before construction began in 1900, the site was expanded to 218 acres. The site plan was developed in 1895 by Frederick Law Olmsted and the architecture firm of Cope and Stewardson. The buildings were based on the medieval courtyards of Oxford and Cambridge colleges.

The timing of this westward move was fortuitous for Washington University because St. Louis was busily preparing for the 1904 World's Fair, to be held in Forest Park. After running out of space in the park, the company organizing the fair leased Washington University's land and the buildings that had been erected. The university received $750,000 in exchange (about $19 million in today's dollars), which it used to further develop the campus and increase its endowment. The campus opened for its first semester in January 1905, immediately following the close of the World's Fair in December.

In its early years, "Wash U" attracted many local students because it was just a streetcar's ride away. In the decades since, the university has continued to grow and is now one of the nation's most highly respected institutions, educating students from across the United States and from around the world. The university encompasses more than 2,300 acres and more than 150 major buildings on its Danforth and Medical campuses, the West Campus and South Campus in Clayton, and additional campuses in the city of St. Louis, University City, and the Tyson Research Center. Enrollment is just under 12,000 full-time students and 2,100 part-time students.

Washington University consistently ranks among the nation's top academic and research institutions. Twenty-two Nobel Laureates have been affiliated with Washington University, including nine who have done the major part of their research at the university. Arthur Holly Compton, who served as chancellor from 1945 to 1953, was the university's first laureate. He won the Nobel Prize in physics in 1927.

Today, Washington University is one of the largest employers of the St. Louis region. Nearly 13,000 faculty and staff members—many of them Clayton residents—are employed by the university.

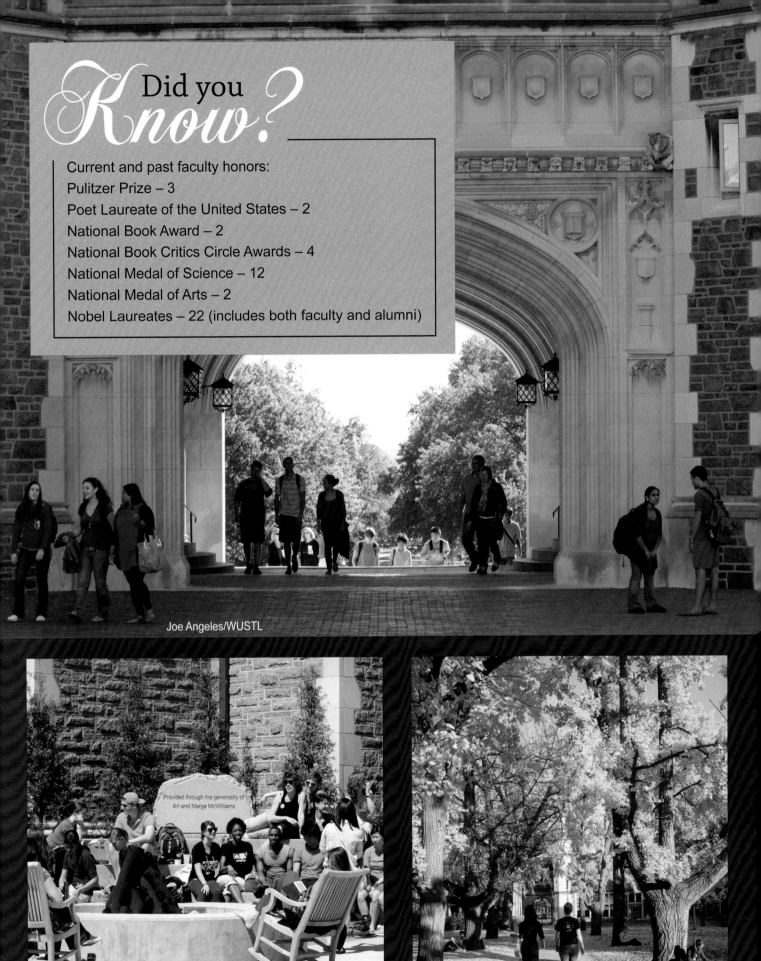

Did you Know?

Current and past faculty honors:

Pulitzer Prize – 3

Poet Laureate of the United States – 2

National Book Award – 2

National Book Critics Circle Awards – 4

National Medal of Science – 12

National Medal of Arts – 2

Nobel Laureates – 22 (includes both faculty and alumni)

Joe Angeles/WUSTL

Provided through the generosity of Art and Marge McWilliams

Joe Angeles/WUSTL

David Kilper/WUSTL

Concordia Seminary

Concordia Seminary is one of the largest seminaries in the United States, providing theological education to Lutheran pastors, missionaries, and leaders. German immigrants founded the seminary in 1839 in Perry County, Missouri. Ten years later, the seminary moved its preparatory division and school of theology to the city of St. Louis.

In 1926, Concordia moved to a wooded seventy-two-acre site purchased from the DeMun estate in Clayton. The campus was designed by Charles Z. Klauder, noted for his work in the Collegiate Gothic style. A crowd of 75,000 from across the country attended the June 13 dedication, and President Calvin Coolidge sent a letter of commendation to be read during the ceremony. The Luther Tower, with its forty-nine-bell carillon, is an area landmark. At its base is the Chapel of the Holy Apostles.

Fontbonne University

Fontbonne University is a four-year Catholic liberal arts institution nestled on thirteen acres at Wydown and Big Bend. Fontbonne was founded by the Sisters of St. Joseph who left France in 1836 and settled in Carondelet, where they taught school in a log cabin. That school grew to be St. Joseph's Academy. Although they started out small, the sisters were thinking big. They wanted to start a college for women.

Archbishop John Glennon selected the site in Clayton. The sisters broke ground in 1924 and held their first classes on the Clayton campus in 1925. In 1928, the first class of eight women graduated with bachelor's degrees. Today, nearly three thousand students from all over the world attend Fontbonne, which began enrolling male students in the 1970s. In 2002, the college changed its status to a university.

Courtesy Fontbonne University

AERIAL VIEW, FONTBONNE COLLEGE,
ST. LOUIS, MISSOURI

PROFILE
THE WILSON SCHOOL

In 1913, a group of Clayton parents collaborated to open a kindergarten for four-year-olds. Mabel Wilson, a respected kindergarten teacher, served as the director and namesake of Wilson School. In 1924, the school was expanded to include three primary grades and a training facility for teachers. In 1960, Wilson School moved to DeMun Avenue and took over the building that previously housed the Community School. The not-for-profit Wilson School Corporation organized in 1968 to oversee the school. Over the decades, Wilson School became a fully accredited elementary school. The building that houses Wilson School, designed by architect William B. Ittner, has been designated as a historic landmark. Wilson School is celebrating one hundred years in 2013.

yearbook lists him as a member of eight clubs and the "Best dressed boy" in the Senior Superlatives section. After graduation, France earned a master's degree in urban studies and a doctorate in public management, and he had a respected career in politics and social service in Chicago.

In recent decades, the School District of Clayton has built a reputation for innovative approaches to education, including an emphasis on teacher training and professional

Captain Elementary School

Glenridge School

development. Dr. Earl Hobbs, who served as superintendent from 1970 to 1991, is credited with implementing programs to keep up with a rapidly changing society. Recognizing that mothers were entering the workforce in larger numbers, Hobbs worked to start before- and after-school care programs and early-childhood instruction that became a model for other districts. Hobbs also volunteered Clayton to be one of the first districts to join the city-county voluntary desegregation program. The district began accepting transfer students before the court-supervised program started in 1983.

Dr. Don Senti, who served as superintendent from 1995 to 2010, noted the deep appreciation Clayton residents have for their schools. "Clayton is unique in that many of our students represent the second and third generation of their families to attend our schools. In fact, many Clayton graduates relocate after college, only to return when they have their own children so they can educate them here," he wrote in a school district history.

Today, Clayton's early childhood center, three elementary schools, middle school, and high school serve a diverse student body of twenty-five hundred who consistently score in the top percentile nationwide on standardized tests. Nearly 100 percent of Clayton High seniors go on to attend two- or four-year colleges after graduation.

In 2011, *U.S. News & World Report* ranked Clayton High School as a silver medal school, as well as No. 85 in the nation for math and science—the highest of any school in Missouri. Those honors, it is worth noting, came one hundred years after nine members of the Class of 1911 made their way through Clayton High to become the school's first graduating class.

Clayton High School
cheerleader and students,
date unknown

Maryland School

Through the Years: The Three Rs in Clayton

1880
Citizens vote to form a school district, build a schoolhouse, and elect directors.

1892
Central School is dedicated; it is best known as the Forsyth School. The building stood on Lee Avenue, immediately south of where the Bracken Building is now.

1894
Crispus Attucks School opens to serve local African-American children. The school is named for the African-American man killed at the Boston Massacre during the Revolutionary War.

1906
The Bellevue School, at Ethel and Bellevue avenues, opens for students who live in the southeastern tip of Clayton.

1908
The second floor of the Forsyth School is converted to Clayton's first high school.

1917
The new Clayton High School opens at 7500 Maryland Avenue with one hundred students in attendance. An addition is built in 1941.

1918
Students of the School District of Clayton take a nine-week "flu vacation" from classes due to the Spanish Flu pandemic.

1921
The Clayton PTA is founded.

The first Clamo Queen is crowned.

Margaret Neff, Clamo Queen, 1929

1922
Christian Brothers College moves into a new school building at University Lane and Clayton Road and will make Clayton its home for eighty years. (After a fire on October 5, 1916, destroyed the private boarding school for boys in north St. Louis, Washington University offered the Smith Academy building to the college for the remainder of the academic year. CBC operated from various schools across the area until 1922.) In 2003, the school relocates to Town and Country. CBC's teams are now nicknamed the Cadets, but they were the Hi-Pointers when the school was located in Clayton's Hi-Pointe neighborhood.

1923
The original Crispus Attucks School is replaced by a brick school building at the same location.

1925
The first junior-senior prom is held.

1926
A Clayton High student writes "Clayton Loyalty," the school song.

1927
DeMun Elementary opens at 6345 Northwood in the DeMun neighborhood.

1929
Glenridge Elementary, 7447 Wellington Way, opens to serve students in the Moorlands neighborhood; a kindergarten house is added in 1954.

A "School Boy Patrol" forms at Bellevue to help policemen direct students crossing streets. Patrols at Forsyth and DeMun follow.

1930
Taylor School opens at 222 North Central Avenue. It closed in 1971 and was demolished.

1931
Forsyth School holds a farewell assembly, attended by current and former students, to celebrate its thirty-nine years of educating the youth of Clayton. The Maryland School opens to replace Forsyth. The building later serves as the Clayton Early Childhood Center.

1939

Meramec Elementary School opens at 400 South Meramec in Davis Place.

1954

Gay School Elementary opens at 301 North Gay Avenue. The building later becomes the Clayton Family Center.

The School District of Clayton integrates. Attucks School closes and is demolished. Clayton High School moves to its new home on Mark Twain Circle.

1962

Bellevue is converted to a seventh-grade center. It is closed in 1965.

1965

Wydown Junior High is built to house grades 7 and 8; it replaces the Hosmer Hall building.

1973

Ralph M. Captain Elementary opens on the former site of the DeMun School.

1974

McMorrow closes and is demolished.

1988

Wydown is renovated and renamed Wydown Middle School.

1932

A frame structure named the McMorrow School opens for elementary students at 1100 McMorrow Avenue. It is later replaced by a brick structure at the same site.

1936

Wydown Junior High opens in the former Hosmer Hall, a private school for girls.

2007

On May 17, the city and school district dedicate a memorial plaque at the site of the old Crispus Attucks School.

2011

A groundbreaking ceremony is held on March 16 for a new Wydown Middle School, to open in 2013.

Chapter Six

A Call to Prayer: Clayton's historic houses of worship

In Clayton's pioneer days, the nearest churches were a long ride away and required considerable horse power—to get to Manchester, Florissant, St. Charles, or even St. Louis. Occasionally, settlers in this part of St. Louis County might attend temporary religious services in private residences, such as the Clayton farm, where Ralph Clayton would host traveling Methodist ministers at his hilltop home. The first churches built in Clayton were often modest structures that were later replaced by the architecturally magnificent houses of worship that live on today in the city's historic neighborhoods.

St. Joseph Catholic Church

The cornerstone for Clayton's first Catholic church, St. Joseph's, was laid in 1885, though its roots in the community date to four decades earlier. In 1842, Ringrose D. Watson, an Irish immigrant who built a successful import business in

St. Louis, deeded land that he owned at Bonhomme Avenue and Price Road in St. Louis County to Bishop Joseph Rosati of the St. Louis diocese "for the sum of $1." Though the price was a token, the property came with a stipulation: It must be used to house a Catholic church or parish school. Accordingly, the cornerstone for St. Martin's was laid that September, and on April 14, 1844, the thirty-six-square-foot brick church was completed and dedicated.

The predominantly French and Irish congregation of St. Martin's included some of the most prominent families of St. Louis County—the Skinkers, Bertholds, and Lindells. The church became the center of a new community, and a gathering place for social interaction and commerce. In 1860, Watson laid out a town plat and named the area Central Village. After Clayton became the county seat, Central Village began to decline.

Archbishop John Glennon at St. Joseph's, 1940

In 1881, St. Louis County donated property at the southwest corner of Maryland and Meramec for the establishment of a Catholic church in Clayton. No church was built in the following years, however, and the Mount Olive Saengerbund, a German singing and social club, acquired the rest of the block around the

Voices

The solid brick St. Joseph's Church has served Clayton for one hundred years, but it had a brush with disaster in its thirteenth year. On March 1, 1925, a Sunday afternoon, a fire broke out in the church, which the Clayton Fire Department attributed to a fallen candle from a side altar. The fire, smoke, and water caused extensive damage to the building; repairs were estimated to cost almost as much as the church's original price. The church lost its pipe organ, three altars, and three stained glass windows. The Clayton community rallied to help St. Joseph's rebuild, including people who were not members of the parish. One of the first to make a contribution was Louis Gutman, of Gutman's Department Store, who was Jewish. In her remembrances of Clayton, Genevieve Neaf shared a memory of the fire:

One of my first memories is when Grandma came to the door all excited saying the Church was on fire. I remember standing in front of Church and someone holding me and everyone worrying. I remember people's reactions more than the fire itself and am now thinking how early children sense tragedy and probably understand a lot more than we realize.

Above: St. Joseph's Church nave

Right: St. Joseph's School, 1929

property. The Saengerbund wanted the entire block, so a deal was worked out. The property deeded by the county for a church was traded to the Saengerbund in exchange for property on the northeast corner of the same intersection.

Father James B. Jackson saw the land acquisition as an opportunity to move St. Martin's parish to the more populous area of Clayton. In 1885, the cornerstone for a frame church and parsonage was built. The new church was dedicated on June 26, 1886, and the parish was renamed St. Joseph's. The ethnic composition shifted to include a higher percentage of German parishioners.

After the turn of the century, the number of Catholic families within the parish boundaries increased markedly, and St. Joseph's outgrew its two hundred-seat church. In June 1912, the cornerstone for a Gothic Revival brick structure was laid in front of a crowd of two thousand people. The Knights of Columbus Choral Club led a parade a half-mile long, and the Clayton brass band performed.

On December 15, Archbishop John J. Glennon dedicated and blessed the new church, which still serves the parish one hundred years later. The project cost St. Joseph's $30,000 (about $696,000 in today's dollars), an amount that the community was willing to help fund. On the Tuesday following the dedication, the church held a bazaar and euchre tournament "at which the financial support of the community was given in liberal measure," according to the *Watchman*.

First Congregational Church of St. Louis

The First Congregational Church of St. Louis is the oldest Congregational church west of the Mississippi River. In 1847, Reverend Dr. Truman Marcellus Post was called to St. Louis to serve as a minister. While he was a Congregationalist, he stipulated that the community be allowed to vote for what type of church they

wanted to establish. Four years later, the members of Reverend Post's temporary church voted to organize a Congregationalist church with Post as their minister. The church held its first service on March 14, 1852, under the name First Trinitarian Congregational Church and Society.

By 1885, the church had moved to its third building in St. Louis, which is now the Grandel Theatre. As development around First Trinitarian continued, the current pastor suggested in 1912 that the church move outside the city limits to a more residential area. Washington University—and therefore Clayton—was the location chosen by a committee.

The Wydown Chapel, at Wydown and University, was constructed and dedicated in 1915. The church was expanded in 1929 and 1947 to accommodate its growing congregation. In 1957, the Congregational-Christian and Evangelical and Reformed churches merged to form the United Church of Christ, and in June 1969, the First Congregational Church was welcomed into the United Church of Christ by the Missouri Conference.

The First Congregational Church of St. Louis, known by its neighbors as "the church with the red doors," celebrated its 150th anniversary in 2001.

Did you Know?

The oldest continuously operating religious station in the world is KFUO-AM, based at Concordia Seminary. The station conducted its first test broadcast in 1924 during the groundbreaking ceremony at Concordia. It is also the oldest-running AM station in the United States.

Mrs. Henri Chomeau: In the winter of 1895-96, harsh conditions made it difficult for Clayton Methodist Church to conduct its activities. Mrs. Henri Chomeau, an original member, kept the church alive by inviting young congregants to her home for religious instruction. From this experience, they formed a Junior League chapter, which went on to hold services at local prisons.

Reverend Dr. Truman Marcellus Post: Reverend Post came to St. Louis in 1847 from Illinois College in Jacksonville, which was known at the time for its staunch abolitionists, including Edward Beecher, brother to Harriet Beecher Stowe. In St. Louis, Post made no secret of his strong antislavery sentiments, even though Missouri was still a slave state, and just across the river in Alton, a mob had lynched abolitionist Elijah Lovejoy five years before. Despite these factors, Post won the approval of his congregants and established an abolitionist Congregational church.

The Reverend Victor Stepka: Father Stepka came to St. Louis in 1904 to establish a Polish parish in the southern part of the city. In 1908, he was appointed pastor of St. Joseph's Church and oversaw the building of the parish's new Gothic Revival church. His tenure at St. Joseph's spanned four decades, and he saw the church through two world wars, the Great Depression, and a fire that severely damaged the church in 1925.

Central Presbyterian Church

Central Presbyterian Church grew from two churches: Central Presbyterian and Clayton Presbyterian, according to Dickson Terry. Clayton Presbyterian originated in July 1890 with the Reverend T. Peyton Walton who preached out of a local home until his congregation decided to build a church. A small frame church was constructed at Coleman (now Brentwood) and Carondelet, and dedicated on May 1, 1892. This church stood for only four years before it was destroyed by a tornado, and a new structure had to be built. In 1913, Clayton Presbyterian moved to a larger building to accommodate its growing congregation.

Central Presbyterian Church was founded on April 18, 1844, with thirty-two members in a small frame building in downtown St. Louis. It was called Fourth Presbyterian Church, before adopting its current name in 1846. Central Presbyterian moved three times—1848, 1873, and 1908—during its nine decades in St. Louis. In 1931, Central merged with Clayton Presbyterian under the name Central Presbyterian. Their new Clayton church—at Hanley Road and Davis Drive—was built in the style of a late-fourteenth-century stone country church.

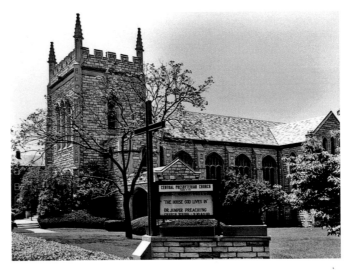

Clayton United Methodist Church

Methodism in Clayton can trace its roots directly to Ralph Clayton. Before the establishment of a Methodist church in the area, circuit-riding preachers conducted services on his Clayton farm. In 1880, the Methodist church in Mount Olive was charged to serve both Clayton and Mount Zion, though the two separated in 1888. The Wilson Chapel, a small frame structure, was built at Bemiston and Sappington (now Shaw Park Drive) in 1882. William Clayton, Ralph's son, served as one of its trustees before entering the ministry.

By 1899, the congregation had almost outgrown their church, so Wilson Chapel was enlarged and remodeled, with the expenses covered by its members. In June 1922, Clayton Methodist moved to a new brick church at the corner of Bemiston and Maryland avenues. The church is now known as The Gathering United Methodist Church.

PROFILE
REMEMBERING "BROTHER CLAYTON"

The flag at the St. Louis County Courthouse flew at half-staff on July 23, 1883, the day Ralph Clayton was laid to rest. It was a fitting tribute for the man who had donated the land it stood on. At ninety-five, Clayton was the oldest—and best-known—resident of the county, according to the local newspapers. His neighbors referred to him fondly as "Brother Clayton." He was a successful farmer who had also run a tannery on his farm for thirty-five years. In his prime, he was an expert marksman—one of the most "unerring riflemen in the West," said the *St. Louis Post-Dispatch*.

Clayton was also remembered for his support of the Methodist religion, which he joined in the 1830s when there were few churches in the county. Traveling Methodist preachers held services on the threshing floor of his barn in the summer and in his home in the winter, according to his obituary in the *Missouri Republican*. The newspaper noted that Clayton had read the Old Testament of the Bible all the way through 110 times.

In 1831, Clayton married Rosanna McCausland, whose family owned a farm near his. Their wedding reception was attended by three hundred people, one of the largest held in the county in those days. The Claytons, who were known for their hospitality, lived in a two-story brick mansion on a hilltop northeast of Brentwood Boulevard and Clayton Road. They had three children. Their son William served as the first clerk of the county court and was later ordained as a Methodist minister.

Samuel United Church of Christ

In May 1905, a group of German immigrants who had settled in Clayton gathered at the courthouse to organize Samuel German Evangelical Church. They acquired Saengerbund Hall, the old German dance and social club, and converted the building into their first church. Services were originally conducted in German.

In 1934, with the national merger of the Evangelical Synod and (German) Reformed Church, the Clayton congregation became the Samuel Evangelical and Reformed Church. In 1948, the congregation moved to a new home, a Norman Gothic building in Clayton Gardens, its current site. The landmark church is now the Samuel United Church of Christ.

Samuel Church, above, in 1910. The original church was in the former Saengerbund Hall building in the 8100 block of Maryland, between North Brentwood and North Meramec Avenue. After World War II, the congregation moved to its current building, left, a Norman Gothic structure at 320 North Forsyth Boulevard.

Hanley Road Baptist Church

In November 1930, a small group of Clayton Baptists petitioned the St. Louis Baptist Mission Board for a church in their city. The board purchased an old ten-room house, the Wenzel home, at Maryland and Hanley to convert to a church. The Hanley Road Baptist Church held services in the remodeled house and Sunday school classes in the former garage. By 1948, the original fourteen members exceeded two hundred, and the church needed a new home. They purchased the Hemingway house, a mansion built in 1903, to use in the interim while building a new church. In 1949, the new Hanley Road Baptist Church was completed. The church is now Hanley Road Church.

Church of St. Michael & St. George

Originally founded as an Episcopal mission congregation on Washington University's campus, the Church of St. Michael and All Angels formed in 1912, just west of Forest Park on Wydown. A parishioner from New York City donated $50,000 to help start the church. The following year, a two-and-a-half-story brick English Gothic church was constructed. Architect James P. Jamieson designed St. Michael in the style of a fourteenth- to fifteenth-century cruciform church. He used materials that reflect those of the buildings that he designed for Washington University. The first services were held in the church on Christmas.

In 1926, St. Michael invited the parish of St. George's Church to join its congregation. St. George's had begun services in 1845 in St. Louis at Locust and Seventh streets. As the population expanded westward, so did the parish, occupying three locations over the next eighty-three years. By 1926, further population decline led St. George's to face dissolution.

In 1928, the two parishes merged under the name the Church of St. Michael & St. George. They used the building of the former Church of St. Michael and All Angels and incorporated elements from St. George's, such as the altar. Both processional crosses are used in the Sunday morning services. To accommodate the influx of parishioners, the church structure was lifted from its foundation, moved, and expanded to twice its previous size, with a capacity for 660 individuals.

PROFILE
JEWISH CONGREGATIONS

Jewish residents of early Clayton belonged to various congregations in the city of St. Louis, including the United Hebrew Temple that relocated in 1927 to Skinker Boulevard opposite Forest Park. That landmark structure, listed on the National Register of Historic Places, is now the Missouri History Museum Library and Research Center. United Hebrew traces its roots to 1837 when two Jewish immigrants organized what is believed to be the first minyan held west of the Mississippi River in a rented room above a restaurant at Second and Spruce streets, now part of the Gateway Arch grounds. The United Hebrew synagogue moved several times before building on Skinker. That construction was initially opposed by some nearby residents, with the litigation ultimately dismissed by the Missouri Supreme Court. In 1977, the congregation moved to its present site at Woods Mill and Conway roads in Chesterfield.

Clayton residents also belonged to synagogues and shuls in University City, including Shaare Emeth, which in 1929 bought and remodeled the Egyptian Building at the corner of Delmar Boulevard and Trinity Avenue. Shaare Emeth was the first Reform Jewish Congregation established west of the Mississippi River. The cornerstone for Shaare Emeth's first temple was laid in June 1867 at Seventeenth and Pine streets in downtown St. Louis. In 1974, the congregation moved from University City to its present twenty-acre site in Creve Coeur, at the corner of Ladue and Ballas roads.

Clayton was home to the Kneseth Israel Congregation for two decades before it merged in 1960 with Brith Sholom in nearby Richmond Heights. Kneseth Israel started when Clayton resident Nolan Dewoskin sought a nearby place to pray, according to a history published by the synagogue. Dewoskin found an empty store to rent on Rosebury near DeMun and enlisted the help of Jewish merchants and salesmen who worked in the Washington Avenue garment district in downtown St. Louis. The congregation later relocated to a four-acre site at 700 South Hanley (now the site of Central Christian School). After the merger, the new congregation—known as Brith Sholom Kneseth Israel, or BSKI—sold the Hanley Road property and moved to 1107 E. Linden in Richmond Heights.

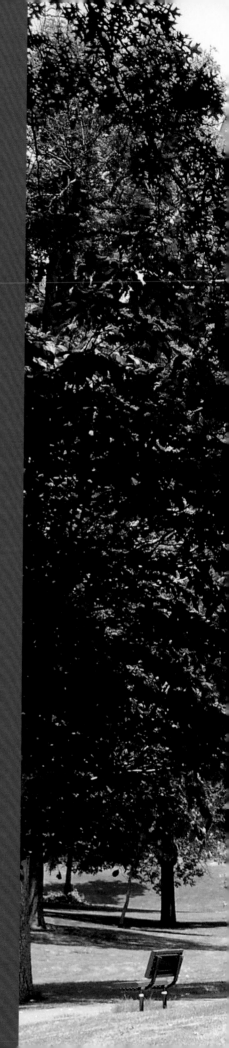

Chapter Seven

For the People: Clayton's award-winning parks grew from hard times

After a colorful parade through the streets of Clayton on May 29, 1937, residents assembled to hear local officials dedicate the new Charles A. Shaw Park and to celebrate the mayor who led the efforts to acquire and develop it. A flag-raising ceremony and music by the Clayton High School band kicked off the party. Mayor Shaw spoke briefly, expressing his thanks for the honor of serving as the park's namesake. Following the oratory, Shaw's nineteen-year-old daughter Betty opened the Olympic-sized pool with an exhibition dive that was followed by a water carnival.

The park cost about $250,000—a huge investment during those lean years of the Great Depression—and it was a marvel to behold on that Saturday afternoon. State-of-the-art recreational facilities contrasted with the park's rolling natural landscape, winding walking paths and canopies of native trees. The 400,000-gallon pool featured 37 underwater lights for nighttime swimming and could hold 700 people, though a limit of 450 had been set to keep it from feeling crowded. When completed, the park would offer tennis courts, a children's playground and recreational center, a baseball field, and a clubhouse.

Shaw Park represented a new gathering place for the community as well as a sign of civic progress—a rebirth of can-do spirit—while the nation was climbing out of its economic pit. The

Clayton, Missouri: An Urban Story

BY THE NUMBERS

Shaw Park swimming fees, 1937

35¢ – Adults

25¢ – Children, under 16

50¢ – Adult lessons

35¢ – Children's lessons

5¢ – Towel rental

Free – Swimming on Tuesday and Thursday mornings for Clayton elementary students

Source: Program of Dedication, The Charles A. Shaw Park, May 29, 1937

impetus for the park had come at the height of the hard times and hinged upon a decision made by the Board of Aldermen just months after Shaw was elected in April 1933. That June, the Republican-leaning aldermen put politics aside and authorized Shaw to apply for a federal grant to fund a host of projects ranging from roads and sewers to a municipal swimming pool. The grants from the Works Progress Administration (WPA)—part of Democrat President Franklin D. Roosevelt's New Deal—were aimed at putting the nation's unemployed back to work.

The souvenir program for the Shaw Park dedication noted the significance of the relief funds, and the principal speaker was Matthew Murray, state administrator of the WPA. According to the *Watchman-Advocate*, Murray told the assembly that the project had given an average of two hundred men employment for eighteen months. "Now this project will pay further dividends in better health and increased recreational facilities for residents of Clayton," Murray concluded.

Shaw Park Tree Top playground, 2010

The establishment of Shaw Park marked the start of Clayton's park system and led to today's award-winning Parks and Recreation Department. In 1934, the Board of Aldermen authorized the mayor to form the city's first park board, and despite the economic times, residents in 1936 voted in favor of a tax to maintain public parks in Clayton. The position of parks and recreation director was created in 1956.

Shaw Park has undergone numerous updates and renovations in its eighty years. In 1960, residents approved a bond issue to build the Clayton Ice Rink, and a new pool and modern bathhouse were constructed in 1967. After renovations in 2003, the pool complex was rededicated as the Shaw Park Aquatic Center. Today, Shaw

Did you Know?

In 1945, Mayor Alfred Kerth and the Board of Aldermen proposed a bond issue to fund construction of an eighty-two-acre airport west of Shaw Park to shuttle passengers to and from Lambert Field. The airport would have had a terminal but no hangars. The plan never got off the ground, and the acreage was used to expand Shaw Park and as the site of the current Clayton High School.

PROFILE
CLAYTON AT PLAY

Shaw Park, the forty-seven-acre jewel of the city's parks and recreation network, is just steps from Clayton's bustling business district. During summer months, residents are drawn to the Shaw Park Aquatic Center and its 50-meter competition pool, dive tank, and children's pool. In winter, they meet at the Shaw Park Ice Rink, first opened in 1961. Scattered about town are nine neighborhood parks. At Oak Knoll Park, the city's second-largest at 14.5-acres, visitors watch for turtles in the pond or ponder 150-year-old Post Oak trees, while at compact .5-acre Wydown Park, the focus is on seasonal gardens.

Did you *Know?*

Clayton hosted the U.S. Outdoor Diving Championships in August 1985. Olympic champion Greg Louganis took first place in the 10-meter platform finals, and the 1- and 3-meter springboard events.

WYDOWN PARK

THEN *and* NOW

Clayton on Ice

Residents of early twentieth-century Clayton fondly recalled ice skating at a place called the Electric Pond near Hanley Road and Wydown Boulevard. The pond drew its name from the fact that it was dug in the late 1800s, while developers were creating an embankment for the roadbed of electric streetcars that would serve the city.

Today, Clayton residents share memories of skating at the Shaw Park Ice Rink that opened in November 1961 and celebrated its fiftieth anniversary in 2011. The rink was designed by Peter Carver and Associates, who created the skating rink for the 1960 Winter Olympics.

Park also includes the Century Garden, ball fields and tennis courts, playgrounds, sand volleyball courts, picnic facilities, and walking and jogging paths. Shaw Park is the oldest and—at nearly fifty acres—the largest of Clayton's parks. It is a lasting tribute to Mayor Shaw's bold plan to build a park during the Depression.

Clayton continues to add to its network of parks that serve the city's neighborhoods, balancing urban growth with the preservation of green space. For many residents, a creative playground and inviting park bench are just a few steps from their doors.

Did you Know?

Dwight Davis, founder of the Davis Cup in tennis, was one of the owners of the Davis estate that sold acreage to Clayton for Shaw Park. Mayor Charles A. Shaw, a real estate developer by trade, worked a deal with the Davis brothers to acquire the land. In addition to the $50,000 paid to the Davises for the acreage, the city also paid for improvements to a subdivision being developed by the Davises.

Clayton, Missouri: An Urban Story

Oak Knoll Park

Clayton's second-largest park—on 14.5 acres of rolling land at the corner of Big Bend Boulevard and Clayton Road—was purchased by the city in 1958. The park is the site of the former Oak Knoll estate, owned by the Rice and Goldman families.

Charles Rice, a St. Louis attorney, purchased the land in 1905 and built a twenty-two-room stone mansion. His brother-in-law Alvin Goldman later built a second home of similar style and scale on the estate. After Goldman's death in 1958, his descendants considered an offer to subdivide the property as a site for about ten houses. Roy Jordan, then chairman of the Clayton City Planning Commission, intervened and convinced the family to sell it to the city for use as a park. Clayton residents approved a bond issue enabling the city to buy Oak Knoll for $350,000.

For more than twenty years starting in 1962, the mansions housed the Museum of Science and Natural History. In 1985, the museum—renamed the Saint Louis Science Center—moved to Forest Park, and the city leased the Rice mansion to the Clayton Child Center, a nonprofit child-care center. After extensive renovation, the St. Louis Artists' Guild moved into the Goldman mansion.

Today, Oak Knoll Park offers neighboring residents picnicking areas, a playground, walking trail, and the Musical Nights concert series in the summertime.

Hanley Park

The city created Hanley Park after purchasing the Historic Hanley House and its nearly one-acre site at 7600 Westmoreland Avenue in the Old Town neighborhood. The wooded grounds feature traditional plantings, including a quince and rose bush that are original to the house and an herb garden typical of traditional formal gardens. In 2012, the city completed the construction of a pavilion that will serve as an outdoor classroom for the numerous groups of students and visitors that come to the museum each year.

DeMun Park

After a series of false starts, the city purchased three quarters of an acre of land in 1973 in the DeMun neighborhood to create DeMun Park. The park, just down the street from popular sidewalk cafes and shops, features a delightful children's playground with creative climbing structures, swings, and a flower garden to attract butterflies. It is popular with families of the DeMun neighborhood as well as residents of nearby Concordia Seminary, Washington University, and the Hi-Pointe/DeMun neighborhood.

Taylor Park

Taylor Park, located at the corner of North Central and Kingsbury in the Old Town neighborhood, is named for the private boys school that operated on the site from 1930 to 1971. The city purchased the land in 1974 for $150,000 and removed the school buildings and landscaped the site. The park's flagpole, refurbished by the Parks Department, honors Taylor students and faculty who served in World War II. It was donated by the Class of 1945. A distinctive yellow gazebo in the park was refurbished to honor Katharine Hoblitzelle, who served on the city's Landscape Advisory Committee.

PROFILE
THE TAYLOR SCHOOL

The Taylor School has now been gone for nearly as long as it existed, but a surviving memorial in Taylor Park pays tribute to the school's faculty, students, and alumni who served their country during World War II.

In 1930, Edgar Curtis "Joe" Taylor, who came to St. Louis to teach at Washington University, opened the private Taylor School at 222 North Central Avenue for boys in grades 6-12. (The school began enrolling girls in 1960.) The Taylor School was housed in a fourteen-room home purchased by Taylor on land that was part of the estate owned by Judson Bemis before Clayton's incorporation. For forty years, the Taylor School provided individualized instruction to students with a curriculum that mirrored teachings in East Coast preparatory schools. Enrollment was capped at fifty students. In 1938, Taylor expanded the school to include new classrooms and a library, and he purchased property at 228 North Central to house faculty. Taylor, originally from New Hampshire, served as the school's headmaster until he retired in 1971 and closed the school.

Clayshire Park

Though small in size, Clayshire Park serves as an example of the park-partner concept, which encourages community involvement in caring for the city's parks. Dedicated in 1997, Clayshire is a triangular park on the eighth-acre tip of a wedge-shaped block in the neighborhood of the same name. Residents did much of the clearing of the site and planted trees and shrubs purchased by the city. The city now cares for the park.

Wydown Park

Wydown Park is a neighborhood gathering place on the north side of Wydown Boulevard near Hanley Road. It started as two vacant lots that had been maintained by residents for years. Children played kickball and baseball on "the lot," and Jewish families would trim the shrubbery in the fall and use the branches to cover sukkah structures during the Sukkot festival. Eventually, the city landscaped the space and installed a fence and benches. The park is known today for its native plants and was recognized by the Missouri Botanical Society for its participation in the Plants of Merit Program. In 2003, *Youth*, a sculpture by Todd Frahm, was placed at the park, inspiring its new nickname as the "acorn park."

Henry Wright Park

Formerly known as Alamo Park, Henry Wright Park is a "pocket park" nestled between two brownstone buildings in the 6400 block of Alamo Avenue in the Hi-Pointe neighborhood. The park was created on the site of an empty lot where a four-unit building once stood. In 2007, residents requested that the park be renamed for Wright, the noted landscape architect and urban planner who platted the Hi-Pointe/DeMun subdivision and other Clayton neighborhoods. Wright served as a trustee of Hi-Pointe before leaving the St. Louis area for New York in 1923. The name change was approved, and the park was updated to include a bronze plaque in Wright's honor.

PROFILE
PLAY BALL!

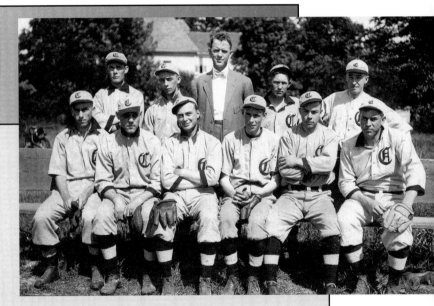

In the spring of 1912, the county seat wasn't yet a city, but it had a semi-professional baseball team—the Claytons—who had won the St. Louis County championship the season before. The baseball games provided entertainment for the town all summer long.

"Don't watch the game from the road side, but enter the grounds and pay your fifteen cents per. It takes money to run the game and your fifteen cents will help toward defraying the expenses," encouraged the *Watchman-Advocate*, as the new season opened on Sunday, April 21. The Claytons were hosting the Mullanphy Club of St. Louis who were "some pumpkins when it comes to the national game" at their park on Bonhomme Avenue. The roster for the home team included returning pitcher Rip Matthews, catcher George Herpel, and "Billy" Autenrieth in center. The Claytons won the season opener 6-4, the newspaper later reported, though the columnist took Herpel to task in the sixth for striking out "as usual."

One hundred years later, a yellowed newspaper clipping about that game still makes for delightful reading in a scrapbook that Herpel's family has shared with the Clayton History Society. Herpel saved all of the baseball columns about his team, along with the irreverent illustrations that accompanied them. In one cartoon, Herpel is squeezed by first base and second base. The caption states, "Piggy Herpel was 'caught' between the bases." In a cartoon captioned "Autenrieth 'muffed' the ball," the ballplayer is attempting to catch a fly ball with a large muff instead of a glove. In that game, Autenrieth redeemed his errors on the field with his bat—and Matthews, the pitcher, was hit by a line drive. The headline was pure baseball poetry: "Autenrieth's Stick Turned the Trick; Rip Knocked Out, Hit on Snout."

Whitburn Park

Whitburn Park was platted in the original design for the Clayshire subdivision; however, when the subdivision opened in 1945, the space was just a grassy median. In 1975, the east end of Whitburn Drive was closed to prevent thru-traffic, leading to the availability of a new green space. The park was dedicated in 2005 after residents voted to designate the open space as parkland, and the Board of Aldermen approved. The park features trees, flowerbeds, benches, and tables and provides a community space for Clayshire residents.

Concordia Park

Concordia Park is located on the grounds of Concordia Seminary, where for more than eighty years, the seminary has allowed its grounds to be enjoyed by its Clayton neighbors. In 1992, the city leased 1.5 acres at the northeast corner of the seminary to provide green space for residents of the DeMun neighborhood. The park also serves the students of Captain School.

The Center of Clayton

From the outset, the School District of Clayton has partnered with the city to provide recreational programs for school-age children. The district bused children to Shaw Park during its first summer in 1937, and its department of physical education provided supervised activities. Those offerings continued to expand, and in 1948 a teen program was added.

In 2000, the Clayton Community Center—which had housed recreational programs and the city's Parks Department offices since 1955—was replaced by The Center of Clayton, an innovative joint initiative of the school district and the city. The 149,000-square-foot center at 50 Gay Avenue is located adjacent to Shaw Park. Its top-notch facilities serve the needs of residents seeking sports, fitness, swimming, recreational, and educational programs and is home to the athletic and physical education programs for Clayton High School. The Center has four gymnasiums, more than 20,000 square feet of aquatic areas, a suspended jogging track, a climbing wall, fitness center, youth activity center, plus aerobic and meeting rooms.

Clayton's Public Art

Clayton's diverse public art by world-renowned artists ranges from classic to modern. The Clayton Art Commission, incorporated in 1988, worked with the city's developers in the selection of works to be installed in new major projects. The commission also partnered with institutions such as the Saint Louis Art Museum, Washington University, and the Gateway Foundation to display works on loan. The city's first commissioned piece—*The Uncertainty of Ground State Fluctuation* by Alice Aycock—was installed in front of The Center of Clayton in 2007.

As part of Clayton's centennial celebration, the Clayton Century Foundation worked with the city to commission *Molecular Bloom with Single Flower*, a steel and bronze sculpture by contemporary artist James Surls that will be installed in 2013 in Shaw Park's Century Garden. The sculpture is a gift from the Centene Charitable Foundation, which pledged

$400,000 for the piece. The Century Garden, located between the ice rink and the swimming pool, has previously displayed *Five Rudders* by Alexander Calder, which was on loan from Washington University, and *Venus Victorious* by Auguste Renoir, which was on loan from the Saint Louis Art Museum.

This is a sampling of Clayton's public art:

* *Uzumaki Curve* by Gerard Tsutakawa
    Carondelet Plaza
* *Dancing Chairs* by Rod Baer
    School District of Clayton, #2 Mark Twain Circle
* *FM6 Walking Jackman* by Ernest Trova
    98 North Brentwood Boulevard
* *Folke Filbyter* by Carl Milles
    Clayton City Hall, 10 North Bemiston Avenue
* *Man on a Horse* by Fernando Botero
    Intersection of Wydown Boulevard and
    Hanley Road
* *Still Point* by Ruth Keller Schweiss
    Ritz Carlton Hotel, 100 Carondelet Plaza
* *The Uncertainty of Ground State Fluctuations*
    by Alice Aycock
    The Center of Clayton, 50 Gay Avenue

Epilogue

by Judy R. Goodman

The Next 100 Years: Clayton looks to tomorrow

Clayton took its time—nearly forty years—before deciding to become a city but has continued moving forward ever since. In 1937, a writer for the *St. Louis Star-Times* offered this explanation for the "the magic" of Clayton's progress:

Claverach Park neighborhood

The swift advance of what was a "courthouse town" suggests magic. The city man, driving through Clayton five years ago and not since, is in for surprises. He will find a changed view. It began when the city man saw opportunity not only for new space for the home, but a topography that lent itself to something more than a checkerboard of uniform lots. Its hills and dales gave variety, well used by architects and buildings.

Out of this natural gift came such rare spots as the beautiful Brentmoors, Forest Ridge, Carrswold, Southmoor, Claverach Park, Country Club Place, Davis Place, Wydown Forest, Hanley Place, Hillcrest and Tuscany Park...

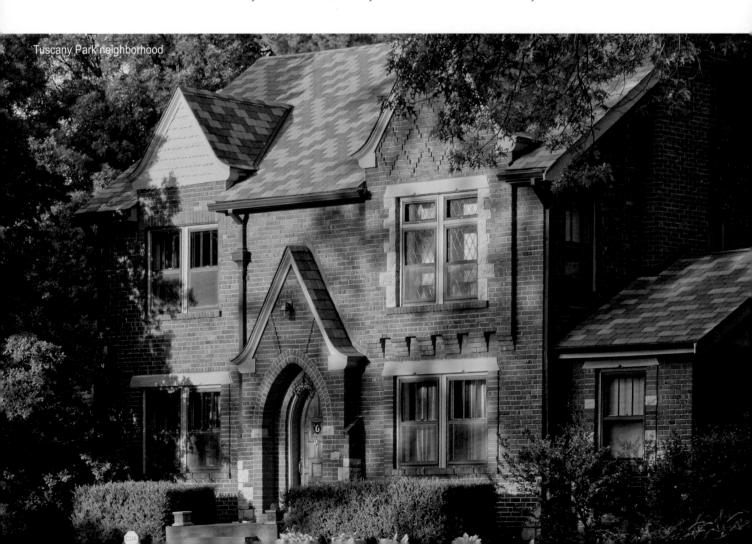
Tuscany Park neighborhood

PROFILE
PLANNING FOR THE NEXT 100 YEARS

In 2007–08, the mayor and Board of Aldermen developed and adopted Vision 2013 as a strategic guide to "building a bright future." Focus areas were identified:

Regional Leadership

- Provide world-class core services
- Maintain and grow status as a leading business center for the region
- Be a leader in environmental initiatives

Partnerships

- Strong partnership with the School District of Clayton
- Strong relationship with institutions and community groups
- Strong support of the Clayton Century Foundation
- Strong ties with neighboring cities

Balance

- Provide quality city services at affordable levels to residents and businesses
- Achieve commercial growth that enriches the city's quality of life, preserves the integrity of residential neighborhoods, and is consistent with the city's comprehensive plan
- Increase dialogue with residential and commercial citizens

In 2012, the city initiated a strategic planning process to determine priorities for the next twenty years and beyond. Titled "C The Future," this comprehensive approach involved reaching out to a wide range of community members to gather broad public input. The process kicked off with a Vision Conference and was followed by an Action Conference. Together, citizens, city leaders, and management staff set the vision, mission, and goals so that Clayton is poised to begin the next one hundred years with a plan that has the investment and support of the entire community.

Today's Gathering Places

Clayton has always been a place to see and be seen.

So many people have fond memories of experiences and iconic gathering places in Clayton, like dessert at Cyrano's, a burger at the Parkmoor, and a movie at the Shady Oak. Clayton is a destination with great places to meet, and new traditions are continually created.

Today, nearly one half million people of all ages gather annually at The Center of Clayton, a hub for sports, recreation, and wellness activities. With eighty-plus award-winning restaurants, the city has become the region's dining mecca. Friends gather at outdoor patios throughout Clayton—for morning coffee at Kaldi's, First Watch, City Coffeehouse, and Starbucks—and for lunch and dinner at restaurants along DeMun, Wydown, Carondelet Plaza, Maryland, and in Clayton's downtown. Every Saturday from May through October, foodies crowd the Clayton Farmers' Market.

During the summer, friends and families gather with picnic baskets and blankets to enjoy live music by local bands at Musical Nights, sponsored by the Clayton Century Foundation, in Oak Knoll Park. The Clayton Chamber sponsors Parties in the Park, attracting a young crowd from around the metropolitan area to downtown Clayton. This original, outdoor, after-work party will celebrate thirty years in 2013.

While providing desirable places for daily gatherings, Clayton has mastered the ability to host celebrated annual events. The Taste of Clayton draws thousands to sample some of Clayton's best restaurants. The Saint Louis Art Fair, produced by the nonprofit Cultural Festivals, recruits two thousand volunteers to assist with this free, three-day event. More than one hundred thousand flock to Clayton streets to experience a celebration of visual and performing arts. The fact that the Taste of Clayton will be in its nineteenth year and the Art Fair in its twentieth speaks to the quality and impact of these memorable events. Clayton's regional appeal continues to grow as the city furthers its commitment to entertainment, cultural, and recreational experiences.

Clayton treasures its historic neighborhoods as vital components of the community and strives to protect its built environment. At the same time, the city incorporates twenty-first-century priorities. Wydown Boulevard reflects this dual commitment. Once the route for city residents to get from downtown St. Louis to St. Louis Country Club, early subdivisions were platted along the way and designed with sensitivity to the natural environment. Originally the streetcar line, Wydown's wide grassy median now features a footpath and lush tree canopy, and the divided boulevard is a key corridor shared by buses, motorists, walkers, joggers, and bikers.

Repurposing older buildings for a new use to meet today's needs is another example of how Clayton supports progress with preservation. For example, the distinctive Famous-Barr Building, at 7425 Forsyth Boulevard, was acquired by Washington University and revitalized as the university's West Campus with several street-level retail spaces. The Shanley Building became business offices, the Seven Gables building is now a hotel, and the Autenrieth Hotel is a business building. Even the long-vacant guard house at the Clayton Road entrance to Somerset Drive was recently converted into an artist's studio.

A major undertaking for the city is the recent transformation of the Heritage Building, at 10 South Brentwood, to house the Clayton Police Department and Municipal Courts. The Colonial Williamsburg–style structure was built in the mid-1950s by Sidney and Jane Studt, who made their home on the top two floors of the six-story office building for more than two decades. The family of Janey Studt Symington sold the building in 1977. When she learned it was purchased by the city in 2009, Mrs. Symington was pleased that this special place of her childhood memories was being preserved. The building features original terrazzo floors, walnut paneling, and brass fixtures, while it reflects the city's progressive leadership as one of the largest solar-powered public projects in the state of Missouri.

Did you Know?

Citizen Survey:

The city of Clayton works with ETC Institute to identify priorities and benchmark performance with other communities. The annual survey is mailed to 1,800 randomly selected households. Since 2009, the city has established 27 high benchmarks in services, from public safety to communications, which include ten new high rankings that were set in 2012. Areas of greatest satisfaction were: quality of public safety services (95 percent satisfaction); quality of parks & recreation programs & facilities (92 percent); and maintenance of city buildings & facilities (91 percent). This survey helps the city to assess operations and establish future goals.

PROFILE
CLAYTON CENTURY FOUNDATION

Ours to Build, Ours to Share: A Prosperous Vibrant City for Generations to Come. In 2008, corporate and residential citizens came together to address the challenges that exist for funding visionary community projects. The Clayton Century Foundation (CCF) was founded as a first-time nonprofit organization to focus on four key passions: parks, public art, history, and sustainability. With a mission to maintain the *Margin of Excellence* that has established Clayton's role as a leading community in the St. Louis region, CCF reached out to philanthropic entities and individuals. CCF provides a tax-deductible civic mechanism for allocating private funds to achieve goals consistent with the city's mission and master plan. By 2012, the CCF had received enough generous pledges to successfully partner with the city to fund significant cultural and recreational improvement projects in Shaw Park, Oak Knoll Park, and Hanley Park. The centennial book, *Clayton, Missouri: An Urban Story* was published with funding provided by the CCF, www.claytoncenturyfoundation.org.

As Clayton recognizes the milestone of one hundred years since incorporation, city leaders and citizens have a rare opportunity to consider everything that came before the lifestyle we know today. So many stories. So many people who made significant contributions. And, so much has changed. Our imagination is aroused, and we are inspired to reflect on the contrasts of past and present, what occurred long ago and what may happen in the future. Let's celebrate our shared sense of community.

Clayton, Missouri: An Urban Story

Mission of the city of Clayton . . . to foster a vital, balanced community composed of outstanding neighborhoods, quality businesses, commercial and government centers, premier educational institutions, and a healthy natural environment through an open, accessible and fiscally responsible government.

CCF BOARD OF DIRECTORS

Cindy Berger
Scot Boulton
Sally Cohn
Gary Feder
Jill Fisher
JJ Flotken
Lotta Fox
Cynthia Garnholz
Ken Goldman

Judy R. Goodman
Lee Hanson
Dan Human
Gary Krosch
Mont Levy
John McCormick
Bob Paster
Cindy Rapponotti
Elizabeth Robb

Janet Rodgers
Steven Rosenblum
Hugh Scott
Jim Sherby
Ben Uchitelle
Cheryl Verde
Bev Wagner
Mark Winings

CCF BUSINESS FOUNDERS

Almonds Restaurant
Al's Wydown Laundry &
    Cleaners
Bauer Soule Garnholz Albin
Brown Shoe Company
Casey Communications, Inc.
Centene Charitable Foundation
Chill Frozen Yogurt
Clayton Chamber of Commerce
Commerce Bancshares
    Foundation
Companion Baking
Dominic Michael Salon

Enterprise Holdings
    Foundation
Enterprise Holdings, Inc.
Faith Berger Art Consultants
Gershman Mortgage
Harbour Group
Husch Blackwell LLP
Kaldi's Coffee
Mark S. Mehlman Realty, Inc.
Moneta Group
Moneta Group Charitable
    Foundation
Protzel's Delicatessen

Robb Partners, Inc.
Ruth's Chris Steak House
Simons Jewelers
Smith, Moore & Co.
The DESCO Group
The Gilroy Law Firm
The Koman Group
U.S. Trust, Bank of America Private
    Wealth Management
Washington University in St. Louis
William T. Kemper Foundation -
    Commerce Bank, Trustee

(June 2012)

CCF FOUNDERS

Lynne and David Anderson
Martha and David Aronson
Beverly and Philip Barron
C. Richard Beard
Sonia and Richard Beard
Cindy and Alex Berger, III
Cathy and James Berges
Brad, Moira, Simone, Jake and Sophie Bernstein
Terry and Richard Bernstein
Brad and Anne Bishop
Joanne and Scot Boulton
Lindsay and Scott Bush
Susan and Chip Casteel
David Charak
Carole and Robert Christie
Sally and Tom Cohn
Fred Cotsworth
Kathianne and David Crane
Andrea Maddox-Dallas and James Dallas
Molly and Chris Danforth
Jeremy Deutsch
Judy and Larry Deutsch
Barbara Eagleton
Marilyn and Bernard Edison
Susan and Peter Edison
Lori and Tim Elliott
Jane Friedrich and Jon Erblich
Robin and Gary Feder
Cheryl and Ed Feutz
Jill and Ron Fisher
Ilene and Burt Follman
Jerome Fondren
Nancy and Steven Fox
Lotta and Jeffrey Fox
Annie and John Gatewood
Prue and Jeff Gershman
Gail and Larry Glenn
James and Angie Glik, in Memory of Gussie Glik
Ann and Bryan Gold
Monica and Dennis Golden

Tricia and Ken Goldman
Linda and Benjamin Goldstein
Judy and Mark Goodman
Claire Halpern and Michael Greenfield
Sheila and Jack Hambene
Carolyn and Chuck Hansen
Michelle and Scott Harris
Lynn Whitmer and Mike Hartmann
Milton Hieken and Barbara Lee Barenholtz
Jennifer and Tom Hillman
Jessie and Craig Hoagland
Nancy and Bill Hobson
Janet and Tom Horlacher
Beatrice and William Human
Kate and Dan Human
Nancy and Richard Hyde
Joanne and Joel Iskiwitch
Robert Johnson
Ashley and John Kemper
Blythe and Peter Kieffer
Amy and Bill, Jr. Koman
Patty and Gary Krosch
William Landau
Kim and Eric Lederman
Lucy and J. David Levy
Mont Levy
Sally S. Levy
Ruth-Ellen and Steve Lichtenfeld
Judi and Sandy MacLean
Phyllis Maritz
Tracey and Bill Marshall
Stephané and John McCormick
David and Ginny McDonald
Diane and Dale Meyer
Laurie Wolff Miller
Jim Reid and Larry Mooney
Evelyn and Eric Newman
Barbara and Michael Newmark
Pam and Cal Nicholson
Traci and Mark O'Bryan
Linda and Joe Orso

Liz and T. Roger Peterson
Carolyn Zacarian and David Poldoian
Julie and Omri Praiss
Nancy and Luke Pritchard
Cindy and Paul Rapponotti
Kristin and James Redington
Jeana and Buddy Reisinger
Elizabeth and Richard Robb
Rosemary and Philip Robbins
Janet and Lee Rodgers
Debbie Zimmerman and Jonathan Root
Andrea and Steven Rosenblum
Steve Schankman
Debbie Chase and Eric Schneider
Karen Branding and Mike Schroeder
Ann and Hugh Scott, III
Judy and Hugh Scott, Jr.
Kathy and Jim Sherby
Jennifer and Walter Shifrin
Jill and Martin Sneider
The Staenberg Family Foundation
Janet and Clarence Turley
Debbie and Hal Tzinberg
Susan and Ben Uchitelle
Cheryl and Nick Verde
Betsy and Tom Wack
Julie and Dan Wagner
Bev and John Wagner
Rita and Scott Waldman
Tom Weil
Scott J. Wilson
Mark and Rula Winings
Gloria and Joe Wotka
Risa Zwerling and Mark Wrighton
Ann and Peregrine Wroth
Karen and Mark Zorensky
Trish and Tom Zupon

Clayton Takes the Lead

1. First Green Power Community in Missouri (only thirty-eight in the United States)

2. Second St. Louis County municipality to adopt a ban on smoking in public places

3. First city, along with Kansas City, in Missouri to adopt an ordinance calling for LEED certification

4. One of only eight in Missouri, the Clayton Police Department serves as a Commission on the Accreditation for Law Enforcement Agencies flagship (only 131 nationally)

5. For twenty-four consecutive years, Clayton's Finance Department has received the Certificate of Achievement for Excellence in Financial Reporting

6. For twenty consecutive years, the city has been designated a Tree City USA

7. Clayton belongs to the elite group of municipalities that maintain Standard & Poor's AAA bond rating